CREATED

for

SUCCESS

Books by Robert Mulindwa

Created for Success
Finding God's Will, Our Purpose,
and True Happiness

Rediscovering Identity
You Are The Image of God

Gain Wisdom, Gain Wealth
The Wise You is the Path to Prosperity

CREATED

for

SUCCESS

Finding God's Will
Our Purpose
And True Happiness

ROBERT MULINDWA

KINGDOM
COME

PUBLISHING

For information about special discounts for bulk purchases or author interviews, appearances, and speaking engagements please contact:

www.RobertMulindwa.com
MulindwaRobert123@gmail.com

First Edition

ISBNs
ISBN Hardcover   979-8-9876653-0-5
ISBN Paperback   979-8-9876653-1-2
ISBN Ebook   979-8-9876653-2-9

Library of Congress: 2023901987

Edited, cover, book and page design by Rodney Miles www.RodneyMiles.com
Cover image of Author © Tucker Photography, www.TuckerPhotograhy.com
Cover image (background, "rockclimbing-2040824") by Pfüderi from Pixabay

*"In whatever man does without God,
he must fail miserably.
Or succeed more miserably."*

— George MacDonald

To every human with inherent potential.

*To every individual predestined
by the Creator.*

*To you the reader, who I believe has what it
takes to realize your full potential.*

*To all who find themselves busy, trying to
get ahead, but ineffective.*

*To the one stuck on the runway of life
desiring to take flight.*

To all who are seeking personal fulfillment.

Acknowledgements

GLORY AND HONOR to the Awesome Majesty and Almighty Devine. As written in the Book of Beginnings (Genesis), God created you and me in His own image according to His likeness. (Genesis 1:26), implying that we are like Him as in being, and are to function like Him. Because He's omnipotent, you and I do have a part of that omnipotent characteristic in us, which translates into the ability to make the invisible, visible. That is to bring forth the unseen into the seen. It's through this inherent characteristic that I was able to unlock and tap into my potential and bring forth this book.

And to my beautiful and beloved wife, this book project couldn't have been possible without your unconditional affection and support. You have always expended effort, over and above, in the upbringing of our children. Thank you.

All worthwhile achievements in life require cooperation from gifted and talented people. The same can be said of this book. A special thank you to Rodney Miles Taber. I am forever grateful to all those who contributed tremendously towards the successful completion of this book. Thank you.

Preface

FOR MOST OF us the word *success* and how we understand it is premised on the culture and school setup we were or are a part of. Important to note is that in school, how well you are doing compared to others is the yard stick for success. And I believe this actually begins with the family, where a system of rewards and punishment is based on how well a child performs compared to their siblings or peers.

This comparative approach then becomes the worldview of what success is to most, if not all of us. The focus is on *impression* instead of *contentment*, resulting in a pursuit of fame, power, money, nobility, reputation, and wealth.

Sadly, this is an erroneous view of what genuine success is. The worldview of success creates a scenario where many a people succeed in the wrong thing. (Yes, there is such a thing as succeeding in the wrong thing.) This is so because true and genuine success is predicated on finding the original reason for existence, the *why* a person exists, so to speak.

Intuitively, the discovery and fulfillment of *purpose* is what true success is about. The good news is , you and I as the image of God already have inbuilt potential within us. This potential consists of the inherent gifts and talents within each of us. However, the only way to realize this potential is when our spirit is under the guidance of the Holy Spirit.

When one comes to understand this, only then can one be truly happy, truly fulfilled. And this is why I have written this book.

To God be the glory, dominion, and Kingdom.

Robert Mulindwa
Nashville, Tennessee
January, 2023

Contents

Introduction

"Dad I don't want to do chemistry. It's economics that I want," I tried to explain to my dad in the principal's office at the beginning of the final two years of my high school.

"Son, I want you to be an engineer and chemistry as a subject is essential," replied my dad.

A tension filled the room as the high school principal looked on in silence. Finally, he broke the silence and turned to my dad and said, "Sir, I know it's with good intention that you desire a future engineering profession for your son, however, we give birth to flesh not the soul. Let him follow his heart."

Up to this point all my academic efforts were driven by the desire to please my dad, but now I felt the desire and courage to do what I was

1

passionate about. I loved economics. Finally, as we headed out of the principal's office, I felt liberated because I stood up for what I believed in. It's crucial to be yourself on the journey to personal fulfillment.

According to a reliable source, the present population of the world is close to 8 billion people. This entails people from different countries and cultures vastly distinct from one another. However, to focus on the differences would be missing the common denominator at the heart of every human walking the face of Earth, which is the desire to succeed. At the heart of every human is the desire to be in control of life's conditions, so to speak. Irrespective of the differences in geographical location, religion, race, or ethnicity, as humans we share feelings of hope, fear, love, joy, and happiness in general. As humans we harbor the inherent desire to be in control of our circumstances or to exercise power or influence over our domain. Intuitively, a feeling or perception of failure is abominable to us as a people. Success is what every human being desires. God created humans to succeed if they obey the physical laws and spiritual principles. True success is about discovering the reason for your existence that will bring about personal fulfillment.

So, what really is success? Per Webster's Dictionary, it's defined firstly as the fact of getting or achieving wealth, respect, or fame; secondly as the correct or desired result of an attempt; and thirdly someone who or something that is successful. Important to note is mankind shares an inherent desire to succeed, however, to be successful means different things to various people from a worldly perspective. For instance, to some it may be completion of studies or starting and owning a business. To others, it may be stability in marriage or getting the job of their dreams. In a country like the United States, the bellwether of capitalism, success is premised on the idea of independence and private ownership. It's all about fame, power, and money as highlighted by media publications like *Forbes Magazine*. However, authentic success is fulfillment of what you were born to do. What you were born to do is the seed that lies in you that requires the right environment to bear fruit.

King Solomon explained it like this:

Many are the plans in a person's heart, but it is the Lord's purpose that prevails.

(Proverbs 19:21, NIV)

Likewise, Isaiah put it this way:

I make known the end from the beginning, from ancient times, what is still to come. I say, My purpose will stand, and I will do all that I please.

(Isaiah 46:10, NIV)

As humans we harbor all sorts of plans, dreams or ideas in our minds, however, what matters is God's desire, intent, and will in our lives. The aforementioned scriptures point out categorically that no matter what we do in life, the purpose of God will forever stand. Whether mankind fulfills it or not, it will never change. Therefore, authentic, original, and real success is the fulfillment of God's purpose. And I am here to report that to live a content and fulfilled life, you must find an answer to the question, "What really is the reason for my existence?" Then spend the rest of your life pursuing it like your life depends on it, because it is paramount.

Chapter 1:

God's Purpose for Man

IN INVESTIGATING THE reason for man's existence, it's imperative to understand the reason why God created mankind in the first place. Using the Kingdom of God Constitution and Law Book[1] as reference, there appeared to be a dialogue among the Holy Trinity the result of which was this:

---

[1] The Bible is the constitution of the Kingdom of God as well as Law Book.

Then God said, Let us make mankind in our image, in our likeness, so that they may rule over the fish in the sea and the birds in the sky, over the livestock and all the wild animals, and over all the creatures that move along the ground." So, God created mankind in his own image, in the image of God he created them; male and female he created them.

(Genesis 1:26-27, NIV)

The inference from this is that mankind is representative of God on Earth with the primary mandate of rulership on behalf of God. We are kings and queens, and God is the King of kings. Moses put it this way:

God blessed them and said to them, be fruitful and increase in number, fill the Earth and subdue it. Rule over the fish in the sea and the birds

in the sky and over every living
creature that moves on the ground.

(Genesis 1:28, NIV)

Let's not forget that it is not anywhere clearly stated or mentioned in scripture that angels were created in the image of God, neither were they given the mandate to rule Earth on God's behalf. This further demonstrates how special a being mankind is. Just like God, so to speak.

To fully appreciate God's purpose for man requires one to answer the question, " What is my identity and origin?" One may be tempted to identify himself/herself by name, race, ethnicity, religion, profession, or geographical location, however, to do so is to misconstrue the essence or crux of the matter. God existed before the beginning, and in the beginning He created the heavens and Earth. All things that were, all things that are, and all things to come, God is. He is the source of all things who spoke the unseen into the seen, the invisible into the visible. On the sixth day of creation, God created man and made animals. God made man from the dirt of Earth just like He did animals, however, He created man by breathing His Spirit into man. Humankind is a spirit having a human experience.

Man has a body, soul, and spirit. Now, all living things—including trees—have a body. The body is the medium through which man processes the world around him through the utilization of the five senses. Intuitively, animals are also capable of this. There exists a lot of similarity between man and animals when you consider the shared features of their external body like limbs, eyes, ears, mouth, and hair as well as their internal organs.

I remember as a nursing student each of us was given a dead preserved cat we used as reference in the laboratory during the Anatomy and Physiology class to familiarize ourselves with the systems of the human body. On the inside a cat is just like a human being, yes indeed. Next is the soul dimension which is the mind, will, and emotions. In the soul we are self-aware, and the soul defines our self-conscious. And I am here to report that animals too have a self-conscious. They are aware of their environment. Humans are uniquely positioned as the only living thing with a spirit through which we cultivate a vertical relationship with God.

In the spirit mankind is capable of fellowship with God. When our spirit communes with the Spirit of God, an alignment is established that enables us to carry out the original mandate of rulership as intended by the Creator. In this way, we reflect the nature, morals, and values of God. We can impact our domain with the will, intent, and purpose of the Creator. On the other hand, failure to operate in spirit pulls us down to the level of animals. This brings about a drive to fulfill the desires of the flesh just like animals do. Many a people when not living in a vertical alignment with the Creator end up suffering addictions like drugs, alcohol, and sex. Therefore, you need the Spirit of God for guidance and teaching to help you in discovering the reason for your existence.

When mankind sinned, he lost the connection to God, and in the process declared independence from the Kingdom of Heaven. Consequently, the Holy Spirit deserted mankind. Man was no longer a representative of God as he fell from rulership. Fortunately, God is a benevolent and compassionate King who then embarked on a mission to restore man into dominion by sending His only son Jesus Christ. Isaiah put it this way:

> *For to us a child is born, to us a son is given, and the government will be on His shoulders. And he will be called Wonderful Counselor, Mighty God, Everlasting Father, Prince of Peace.*
>
> *(Isaiah 9:6, NIV).*

It's very evident here that the Son was to bring a government, and if you remember, the first man Adam fell from rulership of Earth on behalf of God. Therefore, the coming of the Messiah was about restoring man back into Kingdom of Heaven rulership on Earth as well as re-establishing the Holy Spirit connection between man and God. Becoming born again re-establishes the communion between your spirit and God's Spirit.

The Spirit of God teaches and guides you towards fulfillment of God's purpose for your life. The Bible says that God's purpose will always stand no matter what. This implies that whether man fulfills God's purpose or not it never changes. There's no substituting God's purpose. One may come across as successful because he/she is employed with a high-paying job or has a great education, however, this doesn't necessarily imply success or fulfillment.

True success is fulfillment of purpose as intended by God. I believe this could be the reason why even millionaires or billionaires commit suicide; a feeling of emptiness persists when not engaged in what you were born to do. I remember at the height of the 2008 financial crisis there was a German billionaire by the name of Adolf Merckle. It is alleged that when faced with mounting financial pressure, he committed suicide by throwing himself in front of a train near his home. At the time of his death, Forbes ranked him as the 94th richest in the world. Why did Merckle kill himself? His idea of success was the world view.

Many people are captivated by the notion of notoriety and popularity. Instead, man's purpose is predestined by God. The Creator brings man into this world already prepackaged with purpose, implying that true success is fulfillment of the purpose that is already inherent in us.

Think of purpose as a destination. Purpose is destiny. It's a kind of force that draws you towards it. What I am trying to say is that purpose is the quiet voice that keeps talking to you. It's the inner voice that doesn't drown out. Purpose is the pull that keeps tugging at you. When God created mankind, he placed a seed in him. That's why in Genesis He tells us to be fruitful because the seed already exists in us. Unless placed in the right environment that will foster growth, the seed remains unchanged.

So, what's the right environment? Metaphorically speaking the right environment is like digging a hole and burying the seed in fertile soil. This way nutrients from the soil, water, and sun provide the ingredients that foster growth. Within no time the tree shoots out of the ground with branches and leaves and later produces fruit.

Important to note is that the tree never produces fruit for itself, but for others. The seed is the potential—call it purpose or dormant ability— until its acted upon. Now, in reality the right environment is a result of what you listen to, what you watch, or read, and whose company you are in. Too often, many people engage in time-wasting habits like binge-watching TV or movies unnecessarily for hours on end or engaging in other nonproductive engagements.

The success of anything manufactured is directly correlated to the manufacturer. Every manufacturer of a thing is desirous of its success. To ensure success of a product, a manufacturer will run the necessary tests no matter how long, as well as equipping the product with the necessary abilities to fulfill the desired end. For instance, the maker of a computer equips it with the necessary ability and runs the necessary tests to ensure it's in good working order. Finally, when finished with the laptop and certain it will perform the intended purpose, the manufacturer places their logo or brand name on the laptop, their image, so to speak. Important to note is that the manufacturer has their reputation on the line if the product doesn't succeed. For this reason, product fulfillment of intended purpose is in the best interest of the manufacturer as much as it is to the consumer.

Success of the product is actually even more important to the manufacturer than it is to the consumer. To put this in perspective, the Bible says that God created mankind in His own image and likeness, implying that God is the Creator and manufacturer of your life. As the manufacturer, God placed in humankind the ability to accomplish His desired purpose. And like any manufacturer, God desires your success because you are His product. Therefore, God's reputation and glory are on the line when you fail to succeed. God designed mankind to succeed if he/she follows the natural laws and inbuilt spiritual principles. The fundamental requirement is for mankind to create an environment where God's Spirit can reside in him. This way man is in connection with His Creator and able to reflect the nature, morals, and values of God.

A person must accept Jesus Christ as Lord and Savior. This way they are born again to receive the Holy Spirit.

With the Holy Spirit taking residence in man's heart, a person is capable of discernment of the scriptures which promotes a better understanding of God. Apostle Paul expressed it this way:

For who knows a person's thoughts except their own spirit within them? In the same way no one knows the thoughts of God except the Spirit of God. What we have received is not the spirit of the world, but the Spirit who is from God, so that we may understand what God has freely given us.

(1 Corinthians 2: 11-12, NIV)

The Spirit of God opens our eyes of understanding through a relationship with God. This relationship with God is so important because God is the source of man. To create man God had to speak to Himself thereby creating man in His own image and likeness. Without the connections to God, a person is detached from their Source.

Connection to the source is necessary for the success of the object. In essence, it's important for humankind's spirit to be in fellowship with the Holy Spirit. The real secret is in trusting God and keeping God front and center. He should be the focus of our life. Mathew said:

So do not worry, saying, what shall we eat? or What shall we drink? or What shall we wear? For the pagans run after all these things, and your heavenly Father knows that you need them. But seek first His Kingdom and His righteousness, and all these things will be given to you as well.

(Mathew 6:31-33, NIV)

Many a people have settled for less in life and resigned to survival, however, devoting time and effort to seeking closeness to God brings about total transformation. In essence, God is the source of all of things. The Spirit of God makes it possible for a person to harness his potential. Under the guidance of the Holy Spirit, you discover your talents. God's Spirit goes deep into his mind and extracts your purpose and deposits it in your heart. Through discernment God's purpose for your life is revealed by the Holy Spirit.

The Spirit of God then guides and counsels you in living a full and fulfilled life. The Bible says God doesn't live in structures built by hands of men:

However, the Most High does not live in houses made by human hands. As the prophet says: Heaven is my throne, and earth is my footstool. What kind of house will you build for me? says the Lord. Or where will my resting place be?

(Acts 7:48-49, NIV)

To this end, a person's body is a temple for the Spirit of God to take residence. However, the requirement is to be born again which implies to turn away from a life of rebellion and independence to a life of submitting to the will of God. The presence of the Holy Spirit in a person permits man to tap into the mind of God. This is important because the purpose of man lies in the mind of the Creator, hence a connection to God is paramount. The Apostle Paul says:

There are different kinds of gifts, but the same Spirit distributes them. There are different kinds of service but the same Lord. There are different kinds of working, but in all of them and in everyone it is the same God at work. Now to each one the manifestation of the Spirit is given for the common good. To one there is given through the Spirit a message of wisdom, to another a message of knowledge by means of the same Spirit, to another faith by the same Spirit, to another gifts of healing by that one Spirit, to another prophecy, to another speaking in different kinds of tongues, and to still another the interpretation of tongues. All these are the work of one and the same Spirit, and he distributes them to each one, just as he determines.

(1 Corinthians 12:4-11, NIV).

Finding the reason for your existence should be so important in that it graduates from important to an emergency. Why do I say so? It's the destination for your life. You should throw all weight imaginable behind the pursuit of God's purpose for your life. Commitment is a must, followed by persistence together with consistence. Along the journey of life, you will surely encounter failure, setbacks, and challenges, however, it's important to remain steadfast in the Lord God. Per scripture, the steps of a good man are ordered by God. When you choose to submit to Jesus Christ as your Lord and Savior, intuitively you commit to fulfilling your assignment from God. It's the accomplishment of this assignment that yields a sense of personal fulfillment and genuine success.

Chapter 2

The Crux of Faith in God

BEFORE STEPPING INTO one's purpose, an important prerequisite is faith in God. From time to time, you have heard people say, "Keep the faith and trust in God, all will be alright." Normally this response is in times of trials, tests, and challenges, but what really is faith? The Hebrew equivalent for faith is *Emunah*. Emunah implies support, therefore we can count on the Lord's support. The Bible says this about Emunah:

Now faith is confidence in what we hope for and assurance about what we do not see.

(Hebrews 11:1, NIV)

Faith may also be defined as the substance or assurance of things we hope for but have not yet received. Additionally, it's the evidence of that which is not seen. In life, soon or later you come to the acceptance and realization that there are inexplicable things, there are questions whose answers will never be known, there are things out of a person's control, as well as reach, and there are things that cannot be stopped from happening. You know why? God and only God knows. A person must let God be God, which is premised on faith.

When my mom passed away, I struggled to come to terms with the loss. While she was still ill, I prayed to God for her recovery. I couldn't wrap my head around her diagnosis of esophageal cancer that followed just three months after a two-week hospitalization due to surgery for intestinal obstruction. Through-and-through, Mom endured one test after another. Then, when it seemed like she was catching a breather in life, the cancer came knocking. However, what struck me most was the positive attitude and faith in God she kept through it all.

One day she confided in me that she was so grateful to God because her illness couldn't have happened at a better time. Perplexed I asked, "Why?" and her answer was one that has stuck with me up to this day. My Mom was so grateful that God made it possible for coverage of her medical costs, irrespective of her lack of income. This was possible because her children were adults and able to cover the cost of her medical care. Even when it was dark and gloomy, she was still able to pick out a ray of light as well as hope. Talk about faith and confidence in God.

The important lesson I took from my mom's situation was to accept and trust in God no matter what. God should be the focal point of a person's faith, not the actions of God. That is, it's important to anchor our faith not in the acts of God, but God himself. John, son of Zebedee who was the youngest disciple among the twelve, put it this way:

When they found him on the other side, they asked him, Rabbi, when did you get here?

(John 6:25, NIV)

The background to this is that the day prior Jesus fed 5,000 men besides women and children with just five loaves of bread and two fish. And the next day the masses were in search of Him. Jesus answered them:

Very truly I tell you, you are looking for me, not because you saw the signs I performed but because you ate the loaves and had your fill.

(John 6:26, NIV)

Here, we see Jesus pointing out that it's important to seek Him not for the blessings (loaves and fish), but for what He represents which is eternal life. This is corroborated by John:

Then Jesus declared, I am the bread of life. Whoever comes to me will never go hungry, and whoever believes in me will never be thirsty.

(John 6:35, NIV)

As earlier mentioned, it's paramount to make God the fulcrum of one's faith. This promotes confidence and courage to overcome limitations. The devil is counting on you to be dominated by doubt and lack of confidence. When an individual is low on faith, their self-esteem and confidence truncate. Such a person loses the desire to succeed, they lose the will to triumph, and lack the urge to fulfill one's purpose.

Faith in God is so important because it's the light that brightens one's path in the dark. God allows tests and trials in one's life to strengthen and measure our faith in Him. One's faith is directly proportional to the magnitude of the test they overcome. Paul the Apostle put it this way:

No temptation has overtaken you except what is common to mankind. And God is faithful; He will not let you be tempted beyond what you can bear. But when you are tempted, He will also provide a way out so that you can endure it.

(1 Corinthians 10:13, NIV)

You and I are a divine construct by God. He knows how much weight we can bear and won't allow any test beyond the limit you can absorb as an individual. Additionally, out of every trial God will leave an escape route, not to run away but to be able to withstand the challenge.

Consequently, faith comes from hearing the message, and the message is heard through the word about Christ.

(Romans 10:17, NIV)

Hearing the word of God and believing by itself is not enough. One must demonstrate service and obedience to God. Faith is confidence and dependence on God.

One of the scriptures that demonstrates confidence in God is this:

Then the word of the LORD came to him: This man will not be your heir, but a son who is your own flesh and blood will be your heir. He took him outside and said, look up at the sky and count the stars-if indeed you can count them. Then He said to him, so shall your offspring be. Abram believed the LORD, and He credited it to him as righteousness.

(Genesis 15:4-6, NIV).

When God promised Abram a son 25 years went by, but he still believed and had faith in God. God always keeps His promise, however, it's incumbent upon you to be patient and faithful to God. It's crucial that one doesn't waver in the face of trials. It's written in scripture that with faith, you can move a mountain.

The other important dimension to faith is one of dependence upon God. It's imperative that one allows the Holy Spirit to guide them step-by-step. When God created the first man Adam, He placed him in the Garden of Eden. The only prohibition was to never eat the fruit of the tree of the knowledge of good and evil. Now one may ask, *What's wrong with knowing good and evil? Doing evil is certainly bad, but knowing evil shouldn't be a bad thing.*

This tree symbolized two things—life and death. When you abide by the Spirit of God, you accept guidance and counsel on what is good and evil, step-by-step from the Holy Spirit. Contrary to this is independence from God. On the other hand, being content in oneself that you know good and evil, hence no requirement for assistance from God, leads to doing things your own way, banking on the five senses and wit. This is a recipe for disaster. The Bible says this about dependence on God:

For I am the Lord your God who takes hold of your right hand and says to you, do not fear, I will help you.

(Isaiah 41:13, NIV)

Trust in the Lord with all your heart and lean not on your own understanding; in all your ways submit to Him, and He will make your paths straight.

(Proverbs 3:5-6, NIV)

I am the vine; you are the branches. If you remain in me and I in you, you will bear much fruit; apart from me you can do nothing.

(John 15:5, NIV)

The good news for you and me is that when it comes to faith, we don't need to have it in quantities of great proportion. Faith in God is more about concentration, not quantity. It must do more with the potency or power behind it than sheer size. Mathew put it this way:

He replied, because you have so little faith. Truly I tell you, if you have faith as small as a mustard seed, you say to this mountain, move from here to there, and it will move, nothing will be impossible.

(Mathew 17:20-21, NIV)

The background to this story is that Jesus had gone up the mountain with Peter, James, and John the brother of James. While on the mountain He was transfigured before them, after which they returned to the base of the mountain only to find the other nine disciples having failed to heal a boy who was demon-possessed, and suffering from seizures. So, Jesus proceeded to heal the boy after which the nine asked why they couldn't drive the demon out of the boy. In response, Jesus uses a mustard seed analogy in reference to faith. The grain of this seed is so small that it could slip through the fingers of a closed palm or hand, but that's ample faith to overcome the mountains in one's life. What matters is having confidence and trust in God without a doubt.

In his brazen attempt and effort to have dominion over the earth, the fallen cherub called Lucifer wants people to be lacking in confidence. The devil is counting on people to doubt they are blessed and highly favored by God. Satan is banking on you to be wavering and insecure in the belief that you are gifted and not called by God. I am here to report that the devil is a liar and should never be trusted. There's only one God, the benevolent, and compassionate Mighty God.

It's important to focus and ground one's faith in God because He's eternally unchanging. That is the kind of God to hold on to ad infinitum. In life, everything changes, and the only constant is change. To this end, it's wise not to make permanent decisions over temporary situations. Daniel stresses that:

He changes times and seasons; He deposes kings and raises up others. He gives wisdom to the wise and knowledge to the discerning.

(Daniel 2:21, NIV)

Every season in life passes. Nothing comes to stay. Trust in the Lord God.

Believing in God matters a great deal in that doubt and insecurity are not pleasing to God. Trusting in God calls for a laser-focus kind of faith predicated on the El Shaddai[2]:

- Rejected and you still believe,
- broke and still believing,
- lost a job or loved one and still trusting God,
- problems with a teenage child and still believing,
- and so on and so forth.

---

[2] El Shaddai or just Shaddai is one of the names of the God of Israel. El Shaddai is conventionally translated into English as God Almighty — Wikipedia

The Bible says:

And without faith it is impossible to please God, because anyone who comes to Him must believe that He exists and that He rewards those who earnestly seek Him.

(Hebrews 11:6, NIV)

In other words, things like obedience, worship, prayer and so on are lacking where faith is absent. There is a popular adage that you reap what you sow. However, without faith there will be no harvest, even with tithing and other efforts to plant or sow. Therefore, *faith* is paramount and necessary in fulfillment of one's purpose according to God. One must throw all one's weight into seeking God. It's folly to invest effort into seeking other things like money and knowledge instead of placing God front and center.

An important attribute of faith is finding *rest* in God. In pursuit of purpose, it's essential that one finds peace and rest in God. This is so important because the first thing that Adam ever did was to rest.

Adam was created on the sixth day, and rested immediately on the seventh day. This translates to man surrendering all his cares to God. Come hell or high water, come rain or shine, whatever the circumstances in a person's life, it's important to find peace in God. This brings about calmness and composure irrespective of the season in a person's life.

Important to watch out for are the stumbling blocks to faith. These include:

- the devil's tactics,
- a person's past feelings,
- one's level of reasoning,
- negative opinions from others, to name but a few.

Remember, the devil is always plotting for his next victim. This is corroborated in the *Book of Job*, where the Lord said to Satan:

"Where have you come from?"
Satan answered the LORD, "From
roaming throughout the earth,
going back and forth on it."

(Job 1:7, NIV)

The background to this scripture is there was a meeting between God and His angels, Satan joining along. You would expect that the devil was uninvited and crashing the meeting, but that wasn't the case. It's striking that the devil can get audience with God. However, one should take comfort in knowing that irrespective of what the devil does, God protects us.

One summer day as I drove up a street in my neighborhood, I realized my gas tank was about empty, so I pulled up at the next gas station. I proceeded inside, picked up a soft drink and joined the que leading up to the cashier counter. As I waited in line to pay for my gas and drink, I noticed a young male in front of me about twenty years old emptying his pockets one after another as the cashier stood by in patience.

Finally, he came up with a handful of pennies that wasn't enough to meet the cost of his fountain drink. With head down, desolate, and a weary look, the young man stepped to the side, pondering his next move.

I stepped up to the cashier counter to pay for my items and inquired softly of the cashier, "How much does the fountain drink cost?"

"Seventy-five cents," was the reply.

I volunteered to pay for it and handed it over to the young man. This encounter lingered on in my mind, wondering what the reason behind the young man's misery could be. Many a people become overwhelmed by life itself. However, in each person lies greatness in the form of potential. This potential is God's purpose for man. Of importance is keeping God first place and trusting in Him, the result of which is an environment inside you that makes it possible for your spirit to fellowship with the Spirit of God, leading to a revelation and discernment of your purpose.

Fortunately, faith is a gift we receive from God. Through obedience to God as Abraham showed, one's faith will grow. Faith is not something that requires works on our part, but is purely a gift, and we don't have to pay anything in return.

Here is a classic example of what faith entails: Apostle Paul taught that:

If, in fact, Abraham was justified by works, he had something to boast about-but not before God.

(Romans 4:2, NIV)

Simply put, this means that Abraham didn't do anything on his part to be credited as righteous through faith. Paul added:

What does Scripture say? "Abraham believed God, and it was credited to him as righteousness."

(Romans 4:3, NIV)

All Abraham did was believe. Then, Paul says:

Now to the one who works, wages are not credited as a gift but as an obligation. However, to the one who does not work but trusts God who justifies the ungodly, their faith is credited as righteousness.

(Romans 4:4-5, NIV)

You and I are considered righteous through faith in God. God opens our hearts and enlightens our eyes of understanding so that we are convicted in Him as our God. We submit to Him and whole-heartedly believe we need Him. One is justified by faith as righteous, so to speak. This means that God takes away the penalty of our sins and declares us righteous.

Continuing Apostle Paul asserts:

Therefore, the promise comes by faith, so that it may be by grace and may be guaranteed to all Abraham's offspring—not only to those who are of the law but also to those who have the faith of Abraham. He is the father of us all.

As it is written: "I have made you a father of many nations." He is our father in the sight of God, in whom he believed—the God who gives life to the dead and calls into being things that were not.

Against all hope, Abraham in hope believed and so became the father of many nations, just as it had been said to him, "So shall your offspring be."

Without weakening in his faith, he faced the fact that his body was as good as dead—since he was about a hundred years old—and that Sarah's womb was also dead.

Yet he did not waver through unbelief regarding the promise of God but was strengthened in his faith and gave glory to God, being fully persuaded that God had power to do what He had promised.

(Romans 4:16-21, NIV)

This is why Abraham was credited for being righteous. Therefore, anyone who believes in Jesus Christ as Lord and Savior, and believes that He died on the cross to liberate us from sin then through faith, you too are credited with being righteous.

It's imperative to walk by faith, not by sight. For you as an individual, if you are to reach your goals and dreams, faith will be a requirement in stepping out of your comfort zone into the unknown. If you are going to experience personal growth and fulfillment, operating in an environment where the outcomes are unpredictable and things seem out of order, trust and confidence in God are key. This trust and confidence in the Lord God can be nurtured through fervent prayer.

Mark put it this way:

Therefore I tell you, whatever you ask for in prayer, believe that you have received it, and it will be yours.

(Mark 11:24, NIV)

Additionally, in times of challenge and adversity you pray to God to increase your faith, which he grants through the Holy Spirit. Growing one's faith is paramount and it's a lifelong process as one encounters test after test. As I mentioned earlier, one's faith is as strong as the tests encountered. Therefore, praying to God for protection against tests is the wrong prayer. Therefore, as you journey through life, keep the faith in God no matter what.

- When the journey of life seems all an uphill struggle, keep the faith.
- When the bills are high and income is low, keep the faith.
- When feeling rejected and neglected, keep the faith.
- When sick or not in good physical health, keep the faith.
- When you lose a loved one, keep the faith.

- No matter the uncertainty you encounter, keep the faith.

David the Psalmist says:

The Lord makes firm the steps of the one who delights in him; though he may stumble, he will not fall, for the LORD upholds him in his hand.

(Psalms 37:23-24, NIV)

Faith is a requirement in pleasing God, and when you please God, He guides you every step of the way towards your purpose. Along the way one will experience setbacks or falls, but still God has His hand out to lift you up. God knows everyone's end from the beginning. Jeremiah expressed it this way:

Before I formed you in the womb I knew you, before you were born, I set you apart; I appointed you as a prophet to the nations.

(Ipsa loquitar, Latin for "The thing speaks for itself.")

Like any manufacturer of a product, the sole aim of a product is to serve it's intended purpose, to succeed, so to speak. And God's primary purpose for creating man is to manage Earth on His behalf, and succeed in doing so.

Chapter 3:

How You Manage Matters to God

OUR GOD IS one of order, not chaos. When you pay close attention to the anatomy and physiology of the human body with particular focus on the systems that constitute it, you can't help but fill with wonder. How the central nervous system coordinates every other system of the body to function effectively, day-after-day, week-after-week, month-after-month, year-after-year like a well-oiled machine is testament to the existence of God.

Think of the billion neurons in the human brain connected by a trillion synapses functioning in both tandem and independently to orchestrate a symphony of the systems, organs, and cells that make up the human body. Very orderly and meticulous indeed if not mind-boggling. Then look at nature and its ecosystems, how they operate in cycles and circles continuously, yet still in orderly fashion. Now consider the universe with about 200 billion observable galaxies. To put this in perspective, the Milky Way galaxy has eight well-known planets, including Earth. So, this translates into a trillion planets. Yet to date, no report of a planet colliding with another. How is this kind of order possible? There is a God and He's a God of order.

His work, as seen through His creation of Heaven and the universe, exemplifies God. Not only did God do His work of creation in six days, but it was sublime. Moses expressed it this way:

God saw all that He had made, and it was very good. And there was evening, and there was morning— the sixth day.

(Genesis 1:31, NIV)

The essence from this is that work should be rewarding. Work should be something that brings about a sense of fulfillment and honor. In addition, the quality of work reflects the character and integrity of the one who produces it. God created man in His own image and likeness with instructions to rule over His creation. Specifically, He instructed humankind to be fruitful, multiply, replenish, and subdue Earth, as well as having dominion over every living thing on Earth (Genesis 1:26-28).

- To be fruitful speaks to productivity, which is turning potential from the invisible to the visible.
- To multiply is to increase in number of that which is produced.
- To replenish is to supply fully.

49

- To Subdue is to bring under control.

All this translates into *dominion,* which implies sovereignty. In other words, God's reason for creation of humankind was and is rulership of Earth on his behalf.

Important to note is that when God created the heavens and Earth, He waited to allow growth by holding back the rains. The account in Genesis substantiates this:

> *Now no shrub had yet appeared on the earth and no plant had yet sprung up, for the Lord God had not sent rain on the earth and there was no one to work the ground.*
>
> *(Genesis 2:5, NIV)*

The crux of this account is that God didn't allow growth of any kind. The Mighty and Omniscient God had to resolve the conundrum of who was to work the land. To work the land also implies to cultivate. To cultivate implies to foster growth and improve. To foster means to encourage or promote the development of. To promote the development of something that is typically good calls for planning, coordinating, and organizing. This translates into management. Therefore, the main reason why God created man is for management on his behalf. Effective and efficient management translates into dominion of one's domain. This results in progress and accomplishment of the intended purpose. So, we can deduce that God doesn't allow progress and growth where effective and efficient management is lacking.

To be effective is to simply be successful in producing a desired or intended result. Efficiency implies working in a well-organized and competent way, in a manner that maximizes productivity but minimizes wastefulness. Here is a demonstration of efficiency and effectiveness:

Late in the afternoon the Twelve came to him and said, "Send the crowd away so they can go to the surrounding villages and countryside and find food and lodging, because we are in a remote place here."

He replied, "You give them something to eat." They answered, "We have only five loaves of bread and two fish—unless we go and buy food for all this crowd."

(About five thousand men were there.) But He said to his disciples, "Have them sit down in groups of about fifty each."

The disciples did so, and everyone sat down.

Taking the five loaves and the two fish and looking up to heaven, He gave thanks and broke them. Then he gave them to the disciples to distribute to the people.

They all ate and were satisfied, and the disciples picked up twelve basketfuls of broken pieces that were left over.

(Luke 9:12-17, NIV)

In looking up to the heavens first and giving thanks before breaking the bread, Jesus demonstrates that Our Spiritual Father, Jehovah Jireh is the provider of all things, including food. Additionally, in the execution of work or whatever we do, it's toward His glory. Continuing, Jesus gives significance to effective management, by successfully feeding about five thousand men. We see planning, organizing, and coordinating by telling His disciples to sit the crowd down in groups of about fifty. Then efficiency at best is displayed through the maximization of the limited supply of bread and fish to feed everyone present, and later picking twelve basketfuls of leftovers to curb wastefulness.

We can also draw from this example the major qualities of a great manager, like the ability to communicate effectively to get the desired result. A great manager leads by example as we see Jesus not agreeing with the twelve in sending away the crowd, instead He shows the quality of love and caring for others.

Furthermore, Jesus demonstrates the importance of delegating by assigning the twelve disciples tasks. And very important is that we draw inspiration from this situation, that faith in God is important in overcoming limitations.

A big reminder is that God owns everything. Intuitively we own nothing. So it's wiser to store up your treasures in Heaven than on Earth because where your treasures are, your heart will be (Mathew 6:19-20). He entrusted humankind to steward on his behalf.

Since mankind's primary assignment from God is to manage Earth on his behalf, it requires obedience to God. This calls for adhering to the laws of God which places one in alignment with God. And coupled with conviction, trust, and confidence in God, one can benefit from God's favor because faith is pleasing to God.

Jesus said:

I will give you the keys of the Kingdom of heaven; whatever you bind on earth will be bound in heaven, and whatever you loose on earth will be loosed in heaven.

(Mathew 16:19, NIV)

Implying that with guidance of the Spirit of God, obedience translates into accessing the keys, and keys symbolize authority, ownership, control, and power. The primary focus in the execution of our work should be the glory of God, not necessarily for monetary gain. According to Paul's account:

And whatever you do, whether in word or deed, do it all in the name of the Lord Jesus, giving thanks to God the Father through Him.

(Colossians 3:17, NIV)

Here is a management account by Jesus:

He said: "A man of noble birth went to a distant country to have himself appointed king and then return.

"So, he called ten of his servants and gave them ten minas. 'Put this

money to work,' he said, 'until I come back.'

"But his subjects hated him and sent a delegation after him to say, 'We don't want this man to be our king.'

"He was made king, however, and returned home. Then he sent for the servants to whom he had given the money in order to find out what they had gained with it.

"The first one came and said, 'Sir, your mina has earned ten more.'

"'Well done, my good servant!' his master replied. 'Because you have been trustworthy in a very small matter, take charge of ten cities.'

"The second came and said, 'Sir, your mina has earned five more.'

"His master answered, 'You take charge of five cities.'

"Then another servant came and said, 'Sir, here is your mina; I have kept it laid away in a piece of cloth. I was afraid of you, because you are a hard man. You take out what you did not put in and reap what you did not sow.'

"His master replied, 'I will judge you by your own words, you wicked servant! You knew, did you, that I am a hard man, taking out what I did not put in, and reaping what I did not sow?

"'Why then didn't you put my money on deposit, so that when I came back, I could have collected it with interest?'

"Then he said to those standing by, 'Take his mina away from him and give it to the one who has ten minas.' 'Sir,' they said, 'he already has ten!'

"He replied, 'I tell you that to everyone who has, more will be given, but as for the one who has

nothing, even what they have will be taken away.'"

(Luke 19:12-26, NIV).

This is very interesting and enlightening. It's equivalent to the Genesis account where God hands mankind authority to rule or manage on his behalf. Important to note is that every assignment we take on is managing on God's behalf. Whatever we have, we do not own but manage on behalf of God. We are entrusted with authority to carry out managerial duties on behalf of the Creator so to speak. How we perform qualifies us for more favor or resources from the Creator, like the servant who earned ten more from one mina.

This servant exemplified great management. God expects us to not only be productive, but to also multiply resources at our disposal. Great management is pleasing to God and attracts more resources. On the other hand, when we do a shoddy and inferior job of managing resources, it attracts wrath from the Creator. God isn't pleased at all with bad management.

Case in point is the servant who just kept the one mina and never multiplied it. Not only is this displeasing to God, but what we mismanage is *lost*.

Also of importance is the attitude we have in the line of duty. Having a bad attitude like the servant who just laid away the mina in a piece of cloth because he was afraid of his master and considered him a hard man, is not only displeasing to God, but considered wicked before God. Therefore, good management creates trust with God, attracts more favor from God, and places you good in the eyes of the Lord God.

Of great importance is to acknowledge that God owns everything, and we are just stewards. To this end all work should be for the glory of God. At any moment in life, every work at our disposal is an assignment from God. The objective of humankind's work shouldn't be material gain but understanding that the reward is eternal life. The Bible narrates the story of the shrewd manager:

Jesus told his disciples: "There was a rich man whose manager was accused of wasting his possessions.

So, he called him in and asked him, 'what is this I hear about you? Give an account of your management, because you cannot manager any longer.'

"The manager said to himself, 'what shall I do now? My master is taking away my job, I'm not strong enough to dig, and I'm ashamed to beg—I know what I will do so that when I lose my job here, people will welcome me into their houses.'

"So, he called in each one of his master's debtors. He asked the first, 'how much do you owe my master?' 'Nine-hundred of olive oil,' he replied. The manager told him 'take your bill sit down quickly and make it four hundred and fifty.'

"Then he asked the second, 'and how much do you owe?' 'A thousand bushels of wheat' he replied. He told him 'take your bill and make it eight hundred.'

"The master commended the dishonest manager because he had acted shrewdly. For the people of this world are more shrewd in dealing with their own kind than are the people the light.

"I tell you, use worldly wealth to gain friends for yourselves so that when it is gone, you will be welcomed into eternal dwellings.

"Whoever can be trusted with very little can also be trusted with much, and whoever is dishonest with very little will also be dishonest with much. So, if you have not been trustworthy in handling worldly wealth, who will trust you with true riches?

"And if you have not been trustworthy with someone else's property, who will give you property of your own?

"No one can serve two masters. Either you will hate the one and love the other, or you will be devoted to

one and despise the other. You cannot serve both God and money."

(Luke 16:1-13, NIV).

Jesus acknowledges that the people of this world are more shrewd in dealing with their own kind than the people of the light. The essence of this statement is that it's wise to look out for each other, however, Jesus is encouraging people of light to be there for one another. Friendships or relationships that we build with others are more effective in providing security than accumulation of wealth. Therefore, of importance is focus on the future or eternal reward—that is, to store up your treasures in Heaven.

God is pleased if one manages their resources effectively and efficiently. The story also points out an important quality of a good manager, trust. Honesty and trust are so important in a person's work because where they are lacking God holds back on progress. For instance, God watches how you utilize company time. Are you getting to the job on time or not? Are you productive with how you use company time? If you are, then God can bless you with a business of your own, otherwise He won't.

Another example is say you drive a company car. How you handle it could result in you being blessed with a car of your own or not. If you rent someone else's property, and you end up destroying it then God can't bless you with a home of your own.

Evidently, God watches how you manage your resources or finances. And if God entrusts you with little finances or resources, use it wisely and in a generous manner to build lasting relationships. Then He will bless you with bigger resources.

And when you pass the test of effectively and efficiently managing little, not only will you be blessed with more, but also with true riches. What are true riches? True wealth is to be like Jesus Christ. It entails being anointed with the Holy spirit, then having revelations as you read the scriptures and being able to see what others don't see. True wealth is about being humble, speaking with a controlled tongue, loving, and forgiving.

Aldous Huxley, an English writer and philosopher once said; "Experience is not what happens to you. It is what you do with what happens to you." As one trudges along the lonely path of success, youthful idealism collides with the harsh realities of life. The best way to deal with the uncertainty that is inherent in life itself is to expect that things will not always be the same. Patience is a requirement as one encounters setbacks in life. The important thing is to understand that pain is temporary, and nothing comes to stay. After the pain is your reward, if only you hang in there and outlast it.

Emotional stability and adaptability are necessary as they translate into rational choices. With the guidance of the Spirit of God, one progresses stage-by-stage or step-by-step. It's the tortoise approach to success and fulfillment, and not the elevator approach. It is folly to expect that progress towards a desired goal happens fast, a person must learn to trust the process.

The reality is that we all face situations that test our patience, intellect, and emotions. Life itself is challenging as you deal with daily tasks coupled with trying to go after goals and dreams. The Bible says:

> *Do not be anxious about anything, but in every situation, by prayer and petition with thanksgiving present your requests to God. And the peace of God which transcends all understanding, will guard your hearts and your mind in Christ Jesus.*
>
> *(Philippians 4:6-7, NIV)*

Prayers of thanksgiving are an expression of gratitude to God. When you petition God, it involves prayers with specific requests. The essence here is that irrespective of life's trials, one must pray and hand over one's cares to God, trusting God's promises and not wavering in the face of the unknown.

To successfully manage the various aspects of your life calls for self-discipline. My question to you is:

- Do you have self-discipline in your finances?
- Do you have self-discipline in your relationships?

- Do you have self-discipline in your time management?

To have self-discipline requires you to adhere to the physical or natural laws as well as the inherent spiritual principles. God created man in His own image and likeness, implying that part of us should have a character like God's and function like God. This is where the Holy Spirit as a guide makes it possible for humankind to think like God, and act like God.

With self-discipline you think before you speak. With self-discipline you think before you act. When you have self-discipline, your actions are in alignment with your values. Anytime one's thoughts are not in tandem with one's actions, tension and conflict ensue in one's mind.

As I mentioned earlier the spirit is the only dimension that separates humans from animals. Animals too have a body and soul. Self-discipline is to follow what your conscience says, and not what your body wants. Thus you reap the rewards of the spirit. Paul asserted:

But the fruits of the Spirit is love, joy, peace, forbearance, kindness, goodness, faithfulness, gentleness, and self-control. Against such things there's no law.

(Galatians 5:22-23, NIV)

Intuitively, this list includes self-control, call it self-discipline.

If we disregard the guidance and counsel of the Spirit of God and go after the desires of the flesh our life spins out of control. The Bible says:

For the flesh desires what is contrary to the Spirit, and the Spirit what is contrary to the flesh. They conflict with each other, so that you are not to do whatever you want. But if you are led by the Spirit, you are not under the law. The acts of the flesh are obvious: sexual immorality, impurity and debauchery, idolatry and witchcraft, hatred, discord, jealousy, fits of rage, selfish ambition, dissensions, factions, and envy, drunkenness, orgies, and the like. I warn you as I did before, that those who live like this will not inherit the kingdom of God.

(Galatians 5:17-21, NIV)

The desires of the flesh reduce one to the level of animals. Consequences include but are not limited to indebtedness, drug addiction, alcoholic addiction, disease, and crime. When one's life is overtaken by fleshly desires, mismanagement of the various aspects of one's life is the result. God holds back progress under these circumstances. He allows no growth or development under these circumstances.

You are a manager, steward, or caretaker, but not an owner. What am I saying? God is the source of all things, hence the owner of everything. He is the owner of all wealth and riches. Understanding this principle will place you in position to benefit from an endless flow of God's blessings. Jesus said that in this world there are two masters and I am here to report it's not God and the devil, but God and money (Mathew 6:24).

True and genuine success is predicated on choosing to serve God, obedience to God, so to speak. Once born again, you have the Spirit of God living in you and giving you direction. Under this guidance you discover your purpose, and money follows purpose. Tithing is one of schools of money management. Malachi said it like this:

Will a mere mortal rob God? Yet you rob me. But you ask, how are we robbing you? In tithes and offerings. You are under a curse—your whole nation—because you are robbing me.

(Malachi 3:8-9, NIV)

If God is the source of all things, He doesn't need your tithe. However, it is one of the ways we show our love to God. When you don't tithe you are practically robbing God and are dishonest at best. On the other hand, with self-discipline as a result of guidance by the Holy Spirit, tithing aligns you in good standing with God, resulting in a bountiful harvest. The Bible says:

Bring the whole tithe into the storehouse, that there may be food in my house, test me in this, says the Lord Almighty and see if I will not throw open the floodgates of heaven and pour out so much blessing that there will not be room enough to store it.

(Malachi 3:10, NIV)

God says *I dare you to test or challenge me, and I will prove my faithfulness.* In addition, tithing produces good qualities in a person, like being honest, responsible, and accountable.

Listen to me closely, management is the main reason why God created humankind. Effective and efficient management occurs under the guidance of the Spirit of God. It's the Holy Spirit that knows the mind of God and facilitates the bridge between God and man. Once humankind accepts Jesus as Lord and Savior and with faith believes that He died for our sins, then by grace he/she is saved. With this, the Holy Spirit takes residence in our hearts and moment-by-moment directs us to living a purposeful life.

One can focus on the correct priority. Furthermore, the Holy Spirit makes it possible to apply knowledge and understanding thereby making you a wise manager. With wise management God can trust you. Not only that, but God also allows you to grow and progress as an individual due to great management.

The Bible says:

His master replied, well done good and faithful servant! You have been faithful with a few things; I will put you in charge of many things. Come and share your master's happiness!

(Mathew 25:23, NIV)

God is pleased with great management and regards you, faithful and good. Often a time, God entrusts you with little, and successful handling results in being entrusted with much. Therefore, good management attracts more blessings from God. Important to note is that where management is poor God withholds growth and development.

Chapter 4:

The Mind is Indomitable Indeed

REGARDED BY MANY as a great man and visionary, Steve Jobs once said, "Your time is limited, so don't waste it living someone else's life. Don't be trapped by dogma—which is living with the results of other people's thinking. Don't let the noise of others' opinions drown out your own inner voice. And most important, have the courage to follow your heart and intuition." *Heart* and *intuition* here refer to the mind. The primary location of the mind is the brain. The human brain is a super-neural computer with up to billions of neurons connected and communicating through trillions of synapses. To say that it's one of the most complex and fascinating organs is an understatement.

This amazing organ comes with a storage capacity that is as good as unlimited and processes information at a blistering speed of 268 miles per hour. The brain is always active even when you are asleep, so to say that we only use 10 percent of it is a myth. On average the human brain weighs three pounds and only requires sugar and oxygen to function. Twenty-three watts of power, enough to light up a bulb, is generated by this riveting and multiplex structure. The exact location of the mind in the brain continues to baffle science. Why could this be? You can't explain something non-scientific with science. It is mystifying, yet so powerful. The mind can elevate you to heights of greatness or the abyss of misery. It can be so empowering, yet at the same time, enslaving.

Tony Robbins, an American author, tells a story about Stanislavsky Lech—a mind-boggling and wit-defying story of courage. The Nazis broke into the home of Stanislavsky Lech, a Jew, and at gunpoint took the entire family into a waiting crowded train filled with a stench of death and despair.

Once in Krakow, he witnessed his entire family shot, then impatiently waited for his own death. Later, he came to the realization that his death wasn't inevitable, and he embarked on a plan to escape. Little did he know about how to escape, however, against all odds he decided to go through with it. Days turned into weeks and weeks into months. His question to fellow prisoners on how to escape fell on deaf ears, and some avoided him. Undeterred by their lack of cooperation and despair, he confided in himself—*Somehow somewhere, there must be a way to escape this. I will prove to the world that the Nazis are not invincible by escaping from this prison camp.*

Lech was determined not to let his will be crushed by the Nazis. Daily in his mind he would have thoughts like, *I am a man with rights and dignity; Help me God to find a way out of here; There must be a flaw in their security; Today is the day I escape,* and so on. Then one day, he discovered the bodies of the shot victims were piled up someplace. Once the pile was large enough to fill a truck, one showed up to take them away.

Unbeknownst to anyone, Lech stripped naked and laid down in a pile of corpses. A day passed and more bodies were piled over him but he lay still in rotting and foul-smelling human flesh. Finally, the truck arrived, and he was thrown into it with other bodies. Off it went and emptied its contents in an open mass grave. When night came, he climbed out of the grave and ran 25 miles to freedom.

Asking the right question unlocks the power of the human mind.

The Bible says:

> *For as he thinketh in his heart, so is he: Eat and drink, saith he to thee; but his heart is not thee.*
>
> *(Proverbs 23:7)*

Truly, the generosity of a stingy man or miser is false. As he tells you to eat, inwardly he's calculating the cost. This phenomenon can be explained by the nature of the mind, which is two parts: the conscious and subconscious. The *conscious* is the part you are aware of, just as the *subconscious* is running without notice all the time. This subconscious mind is what the scriptures normally refer to as the *heart*.

Any information taken in repeatedly through any of the five senses gets encoded in the subconscious, implying it's permanently stored in the subconscious mind. It's this process that gives birth to habits that are hard to break. Now, the mind mediates between your body and spirit, a medium so to speak. This makes the mind so powerful in that it guides self-control or self-discipline.

Let me put this in perspective for you. When the body receives information through the five senses, it's transmitted to the mind. On receiving the information, the mind processes it and transmits it to the spirit. Once the spirit receives the information, it deciphers the information and sends it back to the mind. In turn the mind communicates to the body what the spirit desires; however, it so happens that the body does not always oblige what the spirit wants. A conflict ensues in the mind, hence a battleground it becomes. In essence, it's the battle for the mind of man.

Why is this? God is counting on mankind to execute His will through man's mind, whilst the devil is after your mind for his agenda. If you are lacking in the Spirit of God, then the mind will disregard whatever the human spirit desires and go with the cravings of the flesh. This is exactly why the mind can empower you if guided by the Holy Spirit or enslave you if you are lacking in the Holy Spirit.

Apostle Paul put it this way:

I thank God through Jesus Christ our Lord. So then with the mind I myself serve the law of God; but with the flesh the law of sin.

(Romans 7:25)

Paul is saying the only way to set aside the desire of fulfilling the sinful cravings of the body is by accepting Jesus as Lord and Savior, becoming born again, and walking by the Spirit of God.

Perhaps you have accepted the way things are in your life, looking on as others pass you by on their way to accomplishment. You wonder if things will ever get any better and maybe you have lost hope and are waiting on things to change. I am here to report there are people who make change happen and there are people who wait for things to change.

The *mindset* is the distinction between the two. It's not the passing of days, weeks, or months that will give birth to the change you desire, it's a new mind. What is holding you back is not others or what people say or think of you. What is holding you back is the enemy within you. What is against your progress is what *you* think and say about you.

You must at some point, say *enough is enough*. You must get tired of eating dirt, and desire getting off the ground. The genesis of your transformation starts with a new way of looking at things. It starts with a new perspective and perception. What I am trying to tell you is that a *new you* calls for the renewing of your mind. The Bible says:

> *Do not conform to the pattern of this world but be transformed by the renewing of your mind. Then*

you will be able to test and approve what God's will is—His good, pleasing and perfect will.

(Romans 12:2, NIV)

Here Paul is urging us to pursue true success which comes about through the guidance of the Spirit of God that lives within us. This connection to God instills in us the ability to think like God. To have a mind of Christ, so to speak. Yes, it's possible to have the mind of Christ. Paul corroborates this:

The person with the Spirit makes judgements about all things, but such a person is not subject to merely human judgements, for who has known the mind of the Lord so as to instruct him? But we have the mind of Christ.

(1 Corinthians 2:16, NIV)

With the Holy Spirit, you have clarity of thought, a clear mind so to speak. A clear mind and clean heart results in walking in the purpose of God, which is the reason for your existence. Clarity of thought through the Spirit of God leads to fulfillment of God's mandate. Among other things, God's mandate for you calls for productivity or fruitfulness, multiplication, replenishment, and subduing of your circumstances. With a mind of Christ, we are called to serve. This type of service requires identifying one's area of gifting—not only identifying, but excelling in your area of gifting, hence bearing fruit. And no tree bears fruit for itself, so it's served to others.

God created mankind with the sole purpose of extending His influence on Earth through mankind. Man is the only creation granted legal authority to rule Earth on God's behalf. Therefore, man is on a mandate to do God's will on Earth through his human will. That's why God breathed into man with His Spirit to serve as a guide and counselor. However, the first man, Adam, declared independence from God via disobedience, and lost the Spirit of God in the process, the result of which was man losing his discernment—that is, a spiritual relationship with the Creator.

This translated into man looking outside of himself for knowledge and understanding. The devil had succeeded in his deceptive mission to subvert man's relationship with God. In doing so, the devil destroyed man's potential to be like God. Since then, Satan's sole mission has been to control man's mind. Why the mind? Because it's with the mind that we serve God. Your mind is a battleground—a battle between serving God or the devil. God chose not to interfere with man's will. Hence, a conundrum for humankind exists where he has a choice between serving God or not.

Fortunately, God is kind and compassionate, so he embarked upon a solution to restore man to his original purpose. So as not to break His own law that requires a spirit to live in a body on Earth, He came to live among men in flesh. I am talking about Jesus the Christ. Not only did Jesus come to destroy the work of the devil, but to restore our potential to be like God, to reestablish man's ability to *discern*.

With the Spirit of God residing in you, you start to think like God. Thinking like God leads you to discovery of your purpose. Your purpose is the work for which you were created. It's the seed within you. Purpose is the destination, and destination is destiny.

The devil is counting on you to leave your house of purpose. The devil is counting on you to doubt you have what it takes to live a fulfilled life. The primary mission of the devil is to control your mind. In the Parable of the Prodigal Son, you notice that the son had all his wants and needs met by his father. However, while under the blessing of his father's house the devil couldn't get to him. So, Satan had to lure him out of his father's house. How did he do it? By manipulating his mind. Once the prodigal son left his father's house (a place of blessing), the devil not only made him lose his inheritance, but his dignity and self-esteem as well. Fortunately, the Lord God is always forgiving, and turning back to Him is the right thing to do.

Important to note is that God made the human body specifically for Him to inhabit. Apostle Paul put it this way:

You say, food for the stomach and the stomach for food, and God will destroy them both. The body, however, is not meant for sexual immorality but for the Lord and the Lord for the body.

(1 Corinthians 6:13, NIV)

Paul implies we don't live to eat, and our purpose shouldn't be about fulfilling the desires of the flesh. The body is much more than a vessel for satisfying fleshly needs or wants, it's in fact a body of Christ and Christ the Holy Spirit lives in the body of those who accept Him as Lord and Savior. In essence, for born-again people, the body is Christ's place of abode. In as much you are to reflect the character of Christ. To be like Jesus calls for renewing of one's mind. Then qualities such as compassion, forgiveness, love, and patience ooze from one's heart. Additionally, one embraces self-control, gentleness, prayerfulness, and serving others. In this way your mind is tailored to the will of God.

Unlike animals which operate on instincts, the human mind processes *ideas*. For instance, when winter comes, bears go into hibernation. Not so for humans. A person should be the architect of the change he or she desires. Laying blame on others, politics, government, taxes, and other things won't yield anything meaningful. Instead, the answer lies in changing one's way of thinking.

Nothing changes until you change. Any desired change occurs through transformation of the mind. For instance, taking on reading as a habit can greatly empower and improve one's condition. Another example could be carefully choosing your relationships. Consciously or unconsciously, the people you relate to impact how you think and behave. Of importance is commitment because without it, you cannot start on anything new. Consistency is then also necessary in bringing about the desired change or improvement.

On the other hand, without clearly defined goals or agenda, the mind is consumed by unimportant details that are not useful, things that are rather interesting but not serious, trifles and trivialities so to speak. You are responsible for harnessing your God-given potential. Many people *react* to life rather than take control of their life.

Success, then, may actually become an obstacle to reaching your full potential as you settle for your last accomplishment.

It's paramount to have *vision* instead of sight, the ability to see beyond the obvious. For instance, when you look at a seed, envision the tree that is trapped within the seed. Intuitively, one should refuse to accept their current circumstances. Like God, you have the potential to create, the potential to turn ideas from the invisible to the visible.

Harnessing of your potential is pleasing to God. When you apply your knowledge and understanding, you are wise. According to the scriptures, when you do harness your potential, you are considered a good and faithful servant (Mathew 25:21). And when you demonstrate the ability to effectively and efficiently use your mind, you will be entrusted with greater assignments.

Interesting to note is that God doesn't interfere with the human mind. Moses said:

When Pharoah let the people go, God did not lead them on the road

> *through the Philistine country*
> *though that was shorter. For God*
> *said, if they face war, they might*
> *change their MINDS and return to*
> *Egypt.*
>
> *(Exodus 13:17, NIV)*

Pay close attention to that statement, "they might change their minds and return to Egypt." It's dumbfounding and astounding that God, the Creator of Heaven and the universe as well as mankind, acknowledges the difficulty involved in changing a person's mind. The background to this story is that the Israelites had been living in captivity for over 400 years. Generation after generation they lived a life defined by servitude as slaves. All they knew was to take orders from their Egyptian masters, such that a mental pattern was engrained in their subconscious mind that dictated their habits and behaviors.

So, God decided to take them another route:

So God led the people around by the desert road toward the Red Sea.

(Exodus 13:18).

No sooner had they left Egypt than Pharoah changed his mind and decided to pursue them. On realizing the Egyptians were coming after them, one Israelite cried out to Moses:

...Was it because there were no graves in Egypt that you brought us to the desert to die? What have you done to us by bringing us out of?

(Exodus 14:11, NIV)

Continuing they said:

Didn't we say to you in Egypt, leave us alone; let us SERVE the Egyptians? It would have been

better for us to SERVE the Egyptians
than to die in the desert!

(Exodus 14:12, NIV)

Notice the question, "Didn't we say to you in Egypt, leave us alone; let us serve the Egyptians?" Alas! Now you comprehend why God didn't take them via the shorter route through the Philistine country. It was because of their servitude mentality, call it the slave mentality which had become their mental programing.

This is the very reason that God created circumstances such that their liberator Moses grew up in Pharoah's palace. This way he was void of the servitude mentality. All in all, it took the Israelites forty years loitering about in the desert before ever crossing into the promised land. Present research shows that in as little as over a month, you could walk from Egypt to Israel. In 40 years, the generation of servitude mentality had died out in the desert, and the younger generation born in the wilderness with a different mentality crossed into the promised land. This could explain why many a people live their entire life without fulfilling their potential. There's need for clear and deliberate effort to renew one's mind to live the desired life.

Understanding how your mind works is important. As a baby or young infant, the conscious mind is not yet operative, implying that the infant is fully reliant on the subconscious mind.

A clear distinction between the conscious and subconscious mind is the ability to allow or not allow information in via the five senses. With the conscious mind, one can think and is able to allow information in through the five senses or to reject it. With the subconscious mind, all information via the five senses is welcome. So, there is no rejection of information at the subconscious level.

What happens over time is that several ideas or a group of mental representations become patterns in the subconscious mind. This formation of patterns happens through repetitive exposure to a specific stimulus, resulting in a mental program that dictates one's habits and behavior. Incidentally, an individual's behavior is a result of the mental patterns in their subconscious mind. This may explain why one's actions may contradict what they believe in.

Too often you find people who are born again, however, their behavior is not reflective of the norms, morals, and values of Kingdom of God living.

Now, you may be asking:

- *How does one achieve their desired living?*
- *How does one start a business and overcome procrastination?*
- *How does one succeed as a spouse?*
- *How does one fulfill their purpose?*

The answer is by reprograming your subconscious mind. For instance, you can take on a new habit of reading books that are tailored towards purpose fulfillment. Repetitive reading of books about purpose fulfillment will lead to a new mental pattern in the subconscious mind. This pattern can further be strengthened by listening to online content tailored toward purpose fulfillment. Now, a mental track will be engrained in the subconscious mind, and new habits or behavior towards purpose fulfillment become part and parcel of one's life.

Chapter 5

Time.
Utilize It or Lose It

RESEARCH HAS IT that on average people spend 90,000 hours of their life at work. That wouldn't be a bad thing, however, the work they are referring to here is a *job*. The true definition of work is what you were born to do, whereas a job is what you are paid to do. Work is the purpose for your existence. Unfortunately, many people spend less of their time on what they are passionate about, and most of their time on trivialities. Imagine if the reverse was true. Many people are preoccupied with daily trivia rather than their *true* occupation.

Untold millions of people make much movement but no progress in their lives, burning up and squandering one of the most valuable if not the most valuable commodities they have. Recent research shows Americans dedicate considerable time swiping left or right on their tablets and mobile phones. (And let's not forget video games!) Today an average American spends almost *five hours watching TV* every day. Unfathomable indeed, and wasteful at best. It is mind-boggling, in the sense that time only goes forward, and never backwards.

Ever wonder why it is taken so lightly?

From the many definitions, dictionary.com defines time as a duration regarded as belonging to the present life as distinct from the life to come or from eternity. It might also be described as the inevitable progression into the future with the passing of present events into the past. It entails the past, present, and future. Time is a commodity that is available to us in equal amount. Irrespective of geographical location, race, ethnicity, social status, everyone has no more than 24 hours, 1440 minutes, or 86,400 seconds available to them in a day.

So, you are who you are depending on how you spend your time. You become who you desire to be depending on how you spend time. Effective management coupled with efficient use of time is paramount if one is to succeed in life. The time passed is irretrievable and not something to be concerned with. You can't reclaim lost time, never. The future is unknown, with no guarantees. Of significance is the present—call it *now*. Now is the time to stop procrastinating and start doing. Now is the time to stop doubting and start believing. I am here to report it's now or never. Approach your life with purpose, strength, tenacity, and sagacity.

Time is life itself. The Bible says:

There is a time for everything, and a season for every activity under the heavens: a time to be born and a time to die; a time to plant and to uproot; a time to kill and a time to heal; a time tear down and a time to build; a time to weep and a time to laugh; a time to mourn and a time to dance; a time to scatter stones and a time to gather them; a time to embrace and a time to refrain from embracing; a time to search and a time to give up; a time to keep and a time to throw away; a time to tear and a time to mend; a time to be silent and a time to speak; a time to love and a time to hate; a time for war and a time for peace.

(Ecclesiastes 3:1-8, NIV)

This implies that the timing of your actions is crucial in the sense that at any given moment the action taken should be appropriate. For instance, speaking is great, but it wouldn't be appropriate to talk back to your parent. To kill is bad, however, in times of war it is duty to defend one's nation. Continuing, King Solomon says:

He has made everything beautiful in its time. He has also set eternity in the human heart; yet no one can fathom what God has done from beginning to end.

(Ecclesiastes 3:11, NIV)

This, implying everything matures at the appropriate time, and often in a way and time that we may not understand why things happen the way they do, but it's important to trust God, no matter what.

Time is all we have, from birth to death and in between. Time is the aggregate of one's life experiences. Every passing second is lost, and it's imperative to spend it on assignments that are in line with God's purpose. Why do I say so? God promises us He has plans for us, that He has plans to prosper us, and plans to give us a future and hope. God asserts that His purpose for our life prevails. Therefore, it only makes sense to be involved in plans that are in line with God's purpose for you.

This, I believe, is effective living as God makes provisions for anyone who is doing His will. However, there are millions of people consumed and preoccupied with plans and business outside of God's will, intent, and purpose. Truly speaking, such people are squandering their time. The good news is that one can redeem time:

- Redeem time by discovering your purpose.
- Redeem time by focusing on a plan.
- Redeem time by focusing on the correct priority—not all priorities are right.
- Redeem time by cultivating relationships that add value to you.

To use one's time wisely is key to living a fulfilled life. There are a couple of scriptures that stress the importance of using time wisely, Old Testament and New Testament, both underscoring the essence of time as outlined below:

*Be very careful, then how you live—
not as unwise but as wise, making
the most of every opportunity
because the days are evil.*

(Ephesians 5:15-16)

*Be wise in the way you act toward
outsiders, make the most of every
opportunity.*

(Colossians 4:5)

*Teach us to number our days, that
we may gain a heart of wisdom.*

(Psalms 90:12)

For I know the plans I have for you declares the Lord, plans to prosper you and not to harm you, plans to give you hope and a future.

(Jeremiah 29:11)

A person's days are determined, you have decreed the number of his months and have set limits he cannot exceed.

(Job 14:5)

Then the Lord said, "My Spirit will not contend with humans forever, for they are mortal; their days will be a hundred and twenty years.

(Genesis 6:3)

Our days may come to seventy years or eighty, if our strength endures; yet the best of them are but trouble and sorrow, for they quickly pass, and we fly away.

(Psalms 90:10)

Wouldn't it be awesome to have all the time in the world? Yet by nature time is fleeting, continuously drifting to the unknown future, living the past in its wake, making the present even more important. Time is sacred. The truth is no one can have time forever, necessitating that you and I carefully and wisely allocate it, lest multiply one's opportunities by zero.

To everyone, time is a precious asset indeed. Hoarding time like money is out of the question. Gathering it or storing it away like grain in a silo is impossible. You would be as likely to catch lightening in a bottle than to amass time. And no wonder, as we are left no choice but to appropriate it at a fixed rate of 24 hours a day. Compared to anything out there, time cannot be stopped, slowed, or restored. Forevermore, time is irreclaimable, irrecoverable, and irreversible.

So, truth be told, the sooner one realizes that time is a master who should be served wisely and diligently, the better. Why do I say so? Because time is the most rigid, inflexible, and unyielding commodity in the world. Accordingly, the abuse of time translates into mismanagement—Ineffective and inefficient allocation of time equals mismanagement in all facets of life, wherefore wise allocation of time is paramount. So, the crux is in what we do with the time we have. Put another way, it's not about how many hours we work, but how much work we put into the hours. It's not about how long one lives, but how one lived.

Intuitively, time should be spent on worthy goals. To this end, time is availed to us daily, and it's up to each of us to utilize it intelligently.

Remember, God has placed eternity in our hearts, and God knows our end from the beginning. God also knows humankind before conception occurs, hence mankind is from eternity and winds back to eternity. The concept of time as we know it begins at birth and ends with death. Now this points to one and only one thing: time is allotted to us for fulfillment of a purpose.

If am to describe eternity as some unending straight line, then time is a finite length on that line. The only reason we come this way is to fulfill God's purpose. God deploys mankind on a mission in time from eternity. He's more interested in the pursuit of the reason for our existence than anything else that we tend to. Prophet Jeremiah implores:

> Before I formed you in the womb I knew you, before you were born I set you apart; I appointed you as prophet to the nations.
>
> (Jeremiah 1:5, NIV)

Life without purpose is lacking in productivity, and time without purpose is a waste. Irrespective of social status, race, or whatever the difference may be, we encounter scenarios, situations, or circumstances that are about the same. For instance, the sun rises and sets daily at specific times around the world. People die every year, people fall sick every year, divorces happen every year, rejection happens every year, people face financial constraints every year, ad infinitum. These events don't segregate between the poor and rich, it's called life. Therefore, to live a desired life is a transformation of the inside rather than the outside. Time and again, you hear people blaming others for their failures. And I am here to report that productive use of time requires inner transformation.

Stop blaming the economy, government, family members, your job, and so on. It takes courage to face oneself. You must look at the person in the mirror and demand a better version of yourself. I am talking about personal development. Acquisition of new skills is an effective use of time in fostering personal development. Another way to improve oneself is through reading more. I am not talking about novels, I mean self-improvement books. Success is a result of wise time management. Day-in-day-out, week-in-week-out, one must do the little things excellently in a consistent manner. Over the years, this will translate into personal fulfillment. Making the most of our time is a requirement.

Despite our inability to stop time or even slow it, a question may arise: "Is the control of time next to impossible?" Fortunately not, because with a deliberate and intentional approach to life, we can harness time. In this regard we can maximize our efforts in a day, week, month, or year. Practically, we achieve more, remain motivated, and inspired.

Important to note is that with respect to time, the opportunities that come our way are limited. Delaying action could cost you a life-changing opportunity. At the same time, mastery of patience is a requirement as you progress towards desired goals. Therefore, preparation is key as you wait for the opportunity, along with being able to recognize the opportunity.

Opportunities in life are limited, hence you must be on alert for when they present themselves. Procrastination should be avoided. Of importance is doing the right and best thing today to enjoy a great tomorrow. Emphasis should be placed on planning. Goal setting follows planning, from which effective decisions and actions are made. This brings about self-control that culminates in a focused and purposeful life. With clear goals and choices, time is wisely invested. In this regard it is not an expense.

There are consequences for being careless and lackadaisical with time. The Book of Proverbs says:

How long will you lie there, you sluggard? When will you get up from your sleep? A little sleep, a little slumber, a little folding of the hands to rest and poverty will come on you like a thief and scarcity like an armed man.

(Proverbs 6:9-11, NIV)

King Solomon again admonishes:

Sluggards do not plow in season so at harvest time they look but find nothing.

(Proverbs 20:4, NIV)

Continuing, King Solomon exhorts:

Do not love sleep or you will grow poor, stay awake and you will have food to spare.

(Proverbs 20:13, NIV)

Squandering of time is tantamount to poverty. Time is the sun around which life revolves. Without time nothing can be achieved, and it's with time all can be achieved. Time is gifted to us daily from a divine reservoir, the supply of which is unfathomable. It's not something we earn, yet we spend it on anything we please, never running into debt as we spend it, and tomorrow is for the taking.

What a gem of a commodity. The rich and poor, kings and subjects, all receive no more than 24 hours a day. Wise use of time correlates to success. Wise use of time must incorporate urgency, importance, and significance. The critical factor is to invest your time, instead of spending it.

What are you going to do with the time you have left?

Chapter 6:

Dedication is Key

During my lifetime I have dedicated myself to this struggle of the African people. I have fought against white domination, and I have fought against black domination. I have cherished the ideal of a democratic and free society in which all persons live together in harmony and with equal opportunities. It's an ideal which I hope to live for and to *achieve. But if needs be, it is an ideal for which I am prepared to die.*

— *Nelson Mandela*

This is an excerpt from the "I Am Prepared to Die" speech given by Nelson Mandela on April 20th, 1964 at the Rivonia Trial[3]. At the time Mandela was being charged in a white, racist, apartheid[4] court with sabotage and the state wanted a death penalty; however, he was sentenced to life in prison. He ended up serving 27 years and later went on to become the first democratically-elected President of South Africa. When you talk of dedication towards a cause, this was it. A life of purpose and dedication, indeed. To live full and fulfilled is premised on dedication to purpose.

Per Merriam-Webster's Dictionary, dedication is defined as a feeling of very strong support for or loyalty to someone or something: the quality or

---

[3] The Rivonia Trial took place in South Africa between 9 October 1963 and 12 June 1964, and led to the imprisonment of Nelson Mandela... —Wikipedia

[4] Apartheid: System of racial segregation based on skin colour common in South Africa —Wikipedia

state of being dedicated to a person, group, cause, etc.

Dedication is a bridge between potential and purpose. It is the unyielding and unchanging focus on fulfillment of purpose. Irrespective of what happens on the outside, irrespective of the circumstances, a dedicated person remains unchanged on the inside. The commitment to the cause is what defines a dedicated person. The arc of life is like a roller coaster ride in an amusement park. At one point you are up, the next point you are down, then a turn to the left or right, you are in or out, and such is life. However, a dedicated person maintains focus through it all.

When it comes to being dedicated to a purpose, Jesus Christ is the perfect model. He was so dedicated to the purpose for which the Heavenly Father assigned Him, that in only three years he accomplished His mission, and yet to this date, over 2,000 years later, His impact in human history is second to none. In our world today there are billions of people who acknowledge Jesus Christ as the Savior. Even one of the biggest non-Christian religions called Islam, recognizes Jesus as a very significant figure. Jesus' impact through the ages to this day is truly one of immense global influence.

Having laser focus and remaining true to a cause translates into genuine success. Genuine success is fulfillment of purpose.

Jesus Christ models focus in the Book of Mathew:

After fasting for forty days and forty nights, He was hungry. The tempter came to Him and said, "If you are the Son of God, tell these stones to become bread." Jesus answered, "It is written Man shall not live on bread alone, but on every word that comes from the mouth of God." Then the devil took Him to the holy city and had Him stand on the highest point of the temple. "If you are the Son of God," he said, "throw yourself down for it is written, He will command his angels concerning you, and they will lift you up in their hands, so that you will not strike

*your foot against a stone." Jesus
answered him, "It is also written do
not put the Lord your God to the
test. ...Away from me, Satan! For it
is written worship the Lord your
God, and serve him only."*

(Mathew 4:2-10, NIV)

Important to note here is how the devil quoted
scripture, and Jesus never refuted the authenticity
of those scriptures, but instead countered the devil
with scripture. Jesus wasn't persuaded by the
outer circumstances of hunger, prominence,
power, or pride. Instead, He was so convicted in His
Spirit that the devil failed miserably in trying to
subvert His purpose.

There's no greater commitment to fulfillment of
purpose than being hungry for forty days and forty
nights yet decline food. This is what being
dedicated to purpose is about, which in turn leads
to success.

The main stumbling block to success is a lack of
objectiveness. Untold millions lead lives without it.
They are preoccupied with minor rather than major

things. It's tragic to live a life without focus on something substantive. Time and again, it's common for individuals to live in the gray area of life, which is not great territory for success. I mean, you are either in the black or the white.

The Book of Revelation implores:

I know your deeds, that you are neither cold nor hot. I wish you were either one or the other! So, because you are lukewarm—neither hot nor cold—I am about to spit you out of my mouth.

(Revelation 3:15-16, NIV)

Indecisiveness is displeasing to God as it is anything but dedication.

- To be dedicated incorporates faith and focus.
- To be dedicated is to live with purpose, and propelled by insight.

- To have the ability to see in the corridors of time is insight.

Irrespective of the turbulence of life, despite the tempest of life, a dedicated person marches on towards the destination. This is walking by faith not by sight. This is the mark of being decisive which is the antidote to procrastination.

Jesus put it this way:

All you need to say is simply yes or no, anything beyond this comes from the evil one.

(Mathew 5:37, NIV)

To procrastinate is to preoccupy oneself with anything but the real issue. Procrastinators are busy in the trifles of life, making a lot of movement but never a step forward. In other words, they spend a great amount of time in the land of *should have*, *could have*, and *would have*. This is a territory surrounded by indecision, compromise, lack of vision, wrong association, and time-wasting until the cows come home. Astonishingly there's a scapegoat for this way of living, it's called "trying to find balance in life," or being a jack-of-all-trades but a master of none.

However, true balance is about remaining stable and steady as you progress toward a destination.

The Book of Deuteronomy exhorts:

This day I call the heavens and the earth as witnesses against you that I have set before your life and death, blessings and curses. Now choose life, so that you and your children may live.

(Deuteronomy 30:19, NIV)

God is giving you a choice to be specific and set your sight on the purpose for which He created you. A life of dedication is a life of purpose. If you walk in the steps of God's purpose for your life, The

Mighty God will back you up. Not only that, but your children will also live.

Choosing is deciding to decide in the face of uncertainty. Usually fear comes about when one sets their sight on fulfillment of purpose. However, dedication is the mustering of courage over fear. Where there is faith, fear abounds. Nevertheless, faith should produce a courage in you that triumphs over fear.

The Apostle Paul implores:

Be on your guard, stand firm in the faith, be courageous, be strong.

(1 Corinthians 16:13, NIV)

To be courageous is to maintain focus and enthusiasm in the face of adversity.

In life there are two kinds of people:

1. those who simply *wish* for things to get better,

2. and those who are *dedicated* to reaching their goals.

Trials, challenges, or adversity are part of the process, however, a dedicated person perseveres through it all. To be dedicated is to remain steadfast, unyielding, and relentless in the pursuit of purpose.

In the Book of James it is asserted:

Consider it pure joy my brothers and sisters whenever you face trial of many kinds, because you know that the testing of your faith produces perseverance. Let perseverance finish its work so that you may be mature and complete, not lacking anything.

(James 1: 2-4, NIV)

With perseverance, patience is in tow. Come hell or highwater, come rain or shine, you press forward without complaining. That is testament to patience which is a prerequisite for dedication. A dedicated individual doesn't get angry or upset when things go wrong as they sometimes will.

The Second Book of Chronicles implores:

But as for you, be strong and do not give up, for your work will be rewarded.

(2 Chronicles 15:7, NIV)

Patience is both forbearance and endurance. It's worth noting that to be dedicated requires the understanding of the concept of *process*. Process involves the steps that will be undertaken towards accomplishment of purpose. Instant success is a myth. Anything of value and worthwhile requires patience, persistence, and determination. Dedication is the fuel that process is premised on. It's when you don't feel like it, but press forward; when nobody is watching, but you press forward. Dedication is a living embodiment of character and integrity. With these two, a person develops staying power.

Character is cultivated in overcoming test-after-test, and then manifested in victory. Character is the ability to remain the same when circumstances around you are changing.

Apostle Paul implores:

Not only so, but we also glory in our sufferings, because we know that suffering produces perseverance; perseverance, character; and character, hope. And hope does not put us to shame, because God's love has been poured out into our hearts through the Holy Spirit, who has been given to us.

(Romans 5:3-5, NIV)

The Spirit of God is vital as it reveals things we can't fathom with world knowledge. When a person is dedicated to fulfillment of God's purpose for his life, the Holy Spirit intercedes on their behalf. Because you are fully dedicated to doing God's will, He will back you up and pick up the bill. The Most High will make provisions to ensure that His purpose in your life is accomplished, if you are dedicated. The Holy Spirit prays for you.

The Book of Romans put it this way;

In the same way, the Spirit helps us in our weakness. We do not know what we ought to pray for, but the Spirit Himself intercedes for us through wordless groans.

(Romans 8:26, NIV)

Continuing Apostle Paul exhorts:

And we know that in all things God works for the good of those who love Him, who have been called according to His purpose.

(Romans 8:28, NIV)

Chapter 7:

Communing with the Person of the Holy Spirit

AMONG HIS LIST of endless titles, he was referred to as:

- CBE (Conqueror of the British Empire),
- His Excellency,
- President for Life,
- Field Marshal Al Hadji Doctor Idi Amin Dada,
- VC,
- DSO,

- MC,
- and Lord of All the Beasts of the Earth.

Not forgetting the title of the "uncrowned King of Scotland," Idi Amin was such an intriguing, fascinating, and feared character that a movie dubbed "The Last King of Scotland" was inspired by his deeds. Talking about deeds, in 1972 he ordered the expulsion of British citizens of Asian origin in their tens of thousands from Uganda.

It is claimed that the actual reason for their expulsion was due to the dream he had, in which Allah revealed to him the need to expel Asians. Idi Amin Dada set a 90-day ultimatum for this to be carried out. Wanton crime, including theft, sexual assault, and all manner of impunity, was perpetrated by his soldiers against Asians during this time. On top of that, throughout his regime hundreds of thousands of innocent civilians were massacred. This was a man with purpose, power, but without Godly principles. Absence of Godly principles is due to lack of guidance by the Holy Spirit.

Multitude of problems in the world are due to humankind operating premised on his senses and wits without the Holy Spirit. Prior to sinning, first man Adam was filled with the Spirit of God; however, disobedience led to the Holy Spirit deserting him. Thousands of years passed, and humankind was living life the best way he knew how. This kind of life was and is characterized by ungodly tendencies like corruption, crime, wars, homosexuality, to name but a few. To save the human race, God embarked on a salvation program headlined by His one and only Son, Jesus Christ.

Until the coming of Jesus Christ, the Holy Spirit was absent from humankind. He couldn't dwell in the unholy bodies of men. From time-to-time, the Holy Spirit descended upon the prophets as they carried out God's instruction, but didn't dwell in them.

The Book of Mark put it this way:

Just as Jesus was coming up out of the water, He saw heaven being torn open and the Spirit descending on Him like a dove. And a voice came from heaven: "You are my son whom I love; with you I am well pleased." At once the Spirit sent him out into the wilderness."

(Mark 1:10-12, NIV)

Therefore, Jesus Christ was man and God at the same time. The sole purpose of Jesus' coming was to restore what first man Adam had lost, and that is the Holy Spirit. This He achieved by dying on the cross, cleansing the human race with His blood, hence making our bodies habitable again by the Holy Spirit. The Spirit of God is that part of the triune which dwells in persons who are "born again" in spirit. So important is the Holy Spirit that a person can never fulfill his/her God-given purpose without the guidance and counsel of the Comforter.

Apostle Paul suggests:

*For who knows a person's thoughts
except their own spirit within them?
In the same way no one knows the
thoughts of God except the Spirit of
God.*

(1 Corinthians 2:11, NIV)

Your purpose as a person lies in the mind of your Creator who is God. You need the Spirit of God which knows the mind of God to commune with your spirit so as to discern what God has in store for you. As humans we are limited by the five senses and our worldly knowledge. To discover God's purpose for our life, we have to connect with the mind of God. This is only possible with the Spirit of God because the Holy Spirit knows the thoughts of God. It's the Holy Spirit that makes us understand what God has in His deep reservoir for us. So, to be truly successful and fulfilled, only happens when you discover with the help of the Holy Spirit, those things about you that are in God.

If God's mind is the deep well, then the Holy Spirit is the bucket that draws from the well and delivers the gift or purpose into your mind, and the

Holy Spirit teaches you all things. The Bible corroborates this as below:

> *But the Advocate, the Holy Spirit, whom the Father will send in name will teach you all things and will remind you of everything I have said to you.*
>
> *(John 14:26, NIV)*

> *But when they arrest you, do not worry about what to say or how to say it. At that time you will be given what to say, for it will not be you speaking, but the Spirit of your Father speaking through you.*
>
> *(Mathew 10:19-20, NIV).*

"Come boldly to the throne (Hebrews 4:16)."

- You don't have to be afraid; the Holy Spirit gives you confidence.

- Don't be afraid about your faith, the Holy Spirit helps you cultivate faith.
- Don't be afraid to trust God because the Holy Spirit helps you grow your trust in God.
- Even when it comes to prayer, the Holy Spirit intercedes on your behalf.

Apostle Paul exhorts:

In the same way the Spirit helps us in our weakness. We do not know what we ought to pray for, but the Spirit Himself intercedes for us through wordless groans. And He who searches our hearts knows the mind of the Spirit, because the Spirit intercedes for God's people in accordance with the will of God.

(Romans 8:26-27, NIV).

In order to be genuinely successful and fulfilled, obedience and adherence to the inherent spiritual principles or natural laws that God put in place is paramount. As our Helper, the Spirit of God guides us in following the spiritual principles and laws that God put in place to govern the functioning of our potential. God being our Manufacturer, He prescribed inherent principles in our design to govern how we can successfully operate.

Additionally, God created each of us for a purpose with potential which speaks to the ability to fulfill purpose. Purpose is God's predestined end for our life. It is the destination. Therefore, the Holy Spirit is pivotal in helping us adhere to the principles so as to succeed.

Success is every person's desire, and the Holy Spirit gives you the power to exert control over your circumstances. Am talking about the power to have dominion over one's life.

The Book of Acts asserts that:

But you will receive power when the Holy Spirit comes on you, and you will be my witnesses in Jerusalem

*and in all Judea and Samaria, and to
the ends of earth.*

(Acts 1:8, NIV)

In the above passage, Jesus promises the twelve apostles reception of the Holy Spirit power. The power he's talking about here is not political or military might; however, it is the transformative power due to the Holy Spirit dwelling in you.

When the Holy Spirit dwells in you, you benefit from the power of dominating your circumstances. You become a witness of Christ, which includes:

- the power to heal,
- the power to cast out demons,
- the power to overcome adversity.

Jesus asserted:

"I have given you the authority to trample on snakes and scorpions

and to overcome all the power of the enemy, nothing will harm you."

(Luke 10:19, NIV)

By snakes and scorpions, Jesus refers to the evil in the world like the devil's demonic attacks, sickness, and even death. God has given us His power through salvation, in that the least in the Kingdom of God has authority to overcome the devil's work.

The Holy Spirit is the influence and authority of God on Earth. The Holy Spirit is the key to experiencing the Kingdom of God's rights and benefits. Below are bible verses to expound on the benefits of the Hoy Spirit:

But very truly I tell you, it is for your good that I am going away. Unless I go away, the Advocate will not come to you; but if I go, I will send him to you.

(John 16:7, NIV)

But when He the Spirit or truth comes, He will guide you into all the truth. He will not speak on His own; He will speak only what He hears, and He will tell you what is yet to come.

(John 16:13, NIV)

But if Christ is in you, then even though your body is subject to death because of sin, the Spirit gives life because of righteousness. And if the Spirit of Him who raised Jesus from the dead is living in you, He who raised Christ from the dead will also give life to your mortal bodies because of His Spirit who lives in you.

(Romans 8:10-11, NIV).

Inside you is the dwelling place of the Spirit of God. In the words of Paul the Apostle:

Don't you know that you yourselves are God's temple and that God's Spirit dwells in your midst? If anyone destroys God's temple, God will destroy that person; for God's temple is sacred, and you together are that temple.

(1 Corinthians 3:16-17, NIV)

To have the most important person on Earth living in you; to have the influence and authority of God dwelling in you; this is mind blowing, but true. The Holy Spirit in a tender and comfortable manner guides your steps towards fulfillment of God's purpose for your life.

Imagine the power of God at your service, and in reality that's exactly what the Holy Spirit is. Important to note, whatever the Spirit of God communicates to you is from Christ Jesus.

Jesus suggests:

"He will glorify me because it is from me that He will receive what He will make known to you. All that belongs to the Father is mine. That is why I said the Spirit will receive from me what He will make known to you."

(John 16:14-15, NIV)

Intuitively, for you to live out your true purpose, it's paramount to adhere to the wise counsel of the Spirit of God. This is necessary because Jesus the Christ lets us know that no one gets to the Father unless through Him. So when the Holy Spirit comes into your life, He taps deep into the thoughts of Christ and reveals them to us. Implying that to be fulfilled calls for knowing what is in the mind of God about you. And the Holy Spirit is the only route to God's mind. Hence fulfillment can never occur in your life because what you are searching for is in God. Second to none is for you to create an environment where the Holy Spirits can live and work in you.

Chapter 8:

There is a Leader Within You

A FEW YEARS ago Oscar-nominated actor Chiwetel Ejiofor (CHOO-ə-tel EJ-ee-oh-for) directed and starred in the movie, *The Boy Who Harnessed the Wind*. Inspired by true events, he tells the story of a 14-year-old Malawian boy, William Kamkwamba (Maxwell Simba). Kamkwamba's story is unbelievable as he beats the odds with zeal and tenacity to find a remedy to the famine that was ravaging his community. The famine was severe and brought about extreme starvation. Kamkwamba asserted that, "One year, our fortune turned very bad. In 2001, we experienced an awful famine. Within five months, all Malawians began to starve to death. My family ate one meal per day at night."

Later, due to inevitable financial constraints, he was forced to drop out of school. However, Kamkwamba resorted to dropping into the school library where he chanced upon a textbook titled *Using Energy*. From the book an idea of creating a windmill developed in his mind. Through improvisation, he utilized a bicycle frame, a pulley, and plastic pipe. First, he made a smaller windmill that was able to power light bulbs, then he went on to make a bigger and taller windmill that pumped water and irrigated gardens. Kamkwamba was so committed, determined, and unyielding in inventing a windmill that saved his entire community as well as the country from the famine.

Kamkwamba went on to receive his college education at Dartmouth College in Hanover, New Hampshire (U.S.A.). Here, he graduated with a bachelor's degree in 2014. Since then he has worked on projects ranging from sanitation in India to prevention of gender-based violence in Kenya.

Like Kamkwamba, each of us was born to do something. Each of us has a calling. We were created and designed by God to fulfill a specific purpose. And like any manufacturer, God equipped us with the ability to fulfill that purpose. Finding that gift is finding oneself. Commitment to producing one's gift as well as excelling in it is the essence of leadership.

Genuine leadership is about discovering the original intent for living, and then throwing all your will behind nurturing and producing that purpose. Genuine leadership can be traced back to the original idea for creating man. In the Book of Genesis, God suggests making man in His own image and likeness. He continues, that man will have dominion over all his creation (Genesis 1:26). To have dominion is to rule or lead. Therefore, God created each one of us to be a leader. To take charge so to speak.

To ensure that man succeeds in this responsibility of leadership, God instilled in man God-like characteristics as well as God-like functioning. Not only that, but God also lays out the steps necessary to being an effective and efficient leader. He instructs mankind to be fruitful, multiply, replenish, and subdue, the result of which is dominion (Genesis 1:28).

You may be wondering, if everyone is a leader, who is to be a follower? A widely distorted view of leadership has led many to believe that to be a leader requires followers. Not so with God. The Creator and Manufacturer of your life views leadership as a service, not a *rulership*.

In the Book of Matthew, Jesus taught that:

"You know that the rulers of the Gentiles lord it over them, and their high officials exercise authority over them."

During this time the Romans were ruling over Judea. The Romans were a mighty superpower at the time who subjected the masses to suppression and oppression. They were authoritative and demanded respect and recognition. Jesus points out that this is not what leadership is about. It is a negative depiction of leadership.

Jesus added:

"Not so with you. Instead, whoever wants to become great among you must be your servant, and whoever wants to be first must be your slave."

A servant is hired to serve while a slave is forced to serve; however, Jesus utilizes these two examples as the model of greatness as well as being second-to-none. To be a leader is about serving. Here Jesus implies that each one of us has a gift to serve to others. You were born with hidden gifts and talents. It's up to you to harness your potential to produce your gift and serve it to the world. Your gift is your purpose. It's what you were born to do, your work, so to speak.

Continuing, Jesus says being a leader is about being a slave. This may boggle your mind; however, Christ Jesus strongly suggests that genuine leadership is premised on becoming a slave to your gift. For instance, becoming a slave to your gift entails investing a great deal of your time towards realization of it. Day-in-day-out, week-after-week, month-after-month, ad infinitum you expend effort towards accomplishment of your God-given purpose.

Important to note:

Just as the Son of Man did not come to be served, but to serve, and to give His life as a ransom for many.

(Mathew 20:28, NIV)

I am here to report that there is a leader trapped in the follower you are. Society, culture, religion, and government have all along molded you into a passive follower. If you recall in Genesis, first man Adam was put in charge of all creation, but not over fellow man. This highlights an important point, that God never intended for man to be governed by external forces or circumstances. Man was designed by God for internal rulership and self-control. Society's main objective is to exert control over man. It's their hope and prayer that you never discover who you really are. The time is now, to find you and reclaim your independence.

Unleash the leader in you. The future you, trapped on the inside is counting on the present you to rise to the occasion. It starts with understanding your true source. Look no further than the Book of Beginnings (Genesis). When God created you, He breathed His Spirit into you. You are from Him, and you possess His characteristics. You have the ability to bring forth ideas into existence. I am telling you that like God, you have omnipotent ability. Am not suggesting that you are equal to God, but underscoring the fact that you have God-like characteristics because He's your source.

Paul implores:

I can do all this through Him who gives me strength.

(Philippians 4:13, NIV)

In the Book of John, Jesus confirms that:

> *"I am the vine, you are the branches. If you remain in me and I in you, you will bear much fruit; apart from me you can do nothing."*

This corroborates that importance of remaining connected to God through His Spirit. It's only through this that a person can bring forth fruit (purpose). And the essence of personal leadership is premised on finding your gift (fruit) and serving it to others.

Jesus adds:

> *"If you do not remain in me, you are like a branch that is thrown away and withers; such branches are picked up, thrown into the fire and burned. If you remain in me and my words remain in you, ask whatever you wish, and it will be done."*
>
> *(John 15:6-7, NIV)*

The key to becoming the leader you were created to be is to remain firmly rooted in your source. Remaining firmly fixed in God through the Holy Spirit connection fosters a fixed or unchanging character that is predicated on correct principles of living. Adherence to the principles nourishes your potential which in turn releases your hidden gift or purpose. To have character is to be immovable and not subject to the whims of the external environment.

Character is the foundation upon which the house of leadership is built. For one to activate their dormant power which leads to fulfillment of purpose, character is a must. With character one is firmly convicted and determined to convert the unseen to the seen.

A common denominator among leaders who rose to the occasion when circumstances demanded, is character. A few names that come to mind include:

- Nelson Mandela,
- Mother Teresa,
- Mahatma Gandhi,
- Dr. Martin Luther King Jr.,
- Abraham Lincoln, to name but a few.

People were attracted to them because of what they stood for, never compromising on their convictions. They were in public what they were in private—the true essence of character. Therefore, it's important to cultivate a belief system that yields values which translate into morals that provide a basis for your character. It's this fixed character that provides a foundation upon which the leader in you can emerge.

Joseph exemplified character and leadership, as shown when Joseph went about his business in Potiphar's house:

One day he went into the house to attend his duties, and none of the household servants was inside. She caught him by his cloak and said, "Come to bed with me!" But he left his cloak in her hand and ran out of the house."

(Genesis 39:11-12, NIV)

Because Joseph was faithful to his master, he refused to compromise on his character and ran away from Potiphar's wife. However, he landed in the King's prison because of the lie paraded by Potiphar's wife against him. Once in Jail, Joseph still kept his faith in God, and his attitude never changed. A true epitome of character.

While in prison, Joseph interacted with the King's chief cupbearer. Years later, the Pharaoh is troubled by a dream which is later interpreted by Joseph after being recommended by the chief cupbearer. Then Pharaoh said to Joseph:

"Since God has made all this known to you, there is no one so discerning and wise as you. You shall be in charge of my palace, and all my people are to submit to your orders. Only with respect to the throne will I be greater than you."

(Genesis 41:39-40, NIV)

Keeping faith in God, refusing to compromise, and remaining unchanged in the face of adversity propelled Joseph into his destiny. Demonstrating a spirit of steadfastness no matter what, speaks to character. It's character that cultivates the leader in you, which leads to self-discovery and personal fulfillment.

To become a leader is not stuff of legends. You and me, and every human being, yet to be born, born, or already born, has a leader in them. True leadership is the essence of self-discovery. Becoming a leader is inspired by subordinating personal gratification to Divine purpose. A true leader's way of life is in alignment with a philosophy premised on discovery of one's God-given gift. After finding this gift, spend the rest of your life nurturing it and then serving it to others.

Chapter 9:

Vision is a Prerequisite for Success

AT THE TURN of the 20th century the race to invent a machine capable of flight and capable of transporting man was the essential endeavor. Unbeknownst to many is that Samuel Pierpont Langley was knee-deep in his efforts to invent the first flying machine, even before the Wright brothers ever attempted to do so. Samuel Pierpont was an astronomer and at some point was an Assistant Professor of Mathematics at Harvard

University. While serving as the Secretary of the Smithsonian Institution, Langley developed an *aerodrome*—call it a *flying machine*. Impressed by his work, the U.S. War Department offered Langley a $50,000 grant that enabled him to further his work on a large scale.

In 1903, with Langley's assistant Charles Manley aboard the aerodrome, their first takeoff ended up in water. The aerodrome had crashed into the river, and Manley lived to see another day. Not to be defeated, Langley launched the aerodrome again on a cold December day in 1903. Much to his chagrin, it crashed into the Potomac River one more time. This was the straw that broke the camel's back, and Langley gave up on trying to fly again.

Meanwhile, the Wright brothers with no college education and working out of a bicycle shop, were closely following the German aviator Otto Lilienthal. After the death of Lilienthal, the two brothers began experimenting with flight.

Choosing Kitty Hawk, North Carolina, due to its strong winds, the Wright brothers set out to launch their flying machine. In close to a minute and over a distance of 852 feet, the Wright brothers had successfully conquered flight, just days after Langley's failure. This is testament to the ingenuity of humankind predicated on imagination and born out of vision. Unique to humankind is the power of imagination which translates into vision. Per Webster's Dictionary, vision is a thought, concept, or object formed by the imagination. It is the manifestation of a thing in the subconscious mind before it is manifested in reality.

Since time immemorial, *vision* has been the fuel behind all breakthroughs in human civilization. Be it in medicine as in the case of Alexander Fleming's discovery of penicillin, or landing the first man on the moon, vision is the sun around which invention and innovation revolve. God never created man just for the sake of it. Man's creation is preceded by purpose. It's with vision that a person discovers their purpose. In finding purpose, a person discovers their reason for being.

Like a sniper focused on a target, an individual with vision is a person on a mission. Whatever lies in the periphery is of little or no concern, what matters is the focus or target. This focus is the reason for being. With insight and sight set on a target, the sniper prepares and channels all his wit and effort towards hitting the target. Likewise when you have vision, your thoughts, ideas, and imagination are directed at fulfillment of God's purpose for your life.

Positive thoughts that translate into ideas are the foundation of vision. The ideas then become imagination.

For as he thinketh in his heart, so is he.

(Proverbs 23:7)

A person's heart is the subconscious mind. The thoughts in the subconscious mind dictate an individual's habits and behaviors. Positive thoughts in the heart, geared towards a person's destiny are the basis for vision. So with vision, a person's choices become few. Vision brings about control— call it self-control in an individual.

With vision, decision-making is easier. Why is this? Because vision fosters discipline which is motivated by purpose that is greater than the other options. So important is the vision that a person organizes their life around values and principles in alignment with their vision. This in turn produces a character in an individual that is unchanging. Character is the bedrock upon which vision is built. David the Psalmist put it this way;

May integrity and uprightness protect me, because my hope, Lord, is in you.

(Psalms 25:21, NIV)

Where there is vision, a person puts off personal pleasure. Where there is vision, there is no room for distraction. Actually, you can equally say that with focus on purpose fulfillment, tunnel vision is the result.

King Solomon implored:

Where there is no revelation, people cast off restraint; but blessed is the one who heeds wisdom's instruction.

(Proverbs 29:18, NIV)

The implication from this scripture is that when an individual is unrestrained, their life is defined by lack of focus. Such a person is easily distracted by the apparent lack of attention on one particular thing, but rather they have too many rods in the fire. Success in life calls for building mastery in a specific area of excellence.

To have vision is the ability to imagine and see things clearly before they play out in the natural. A visionary is able to see the unseen before it manifests in reality.

The Bible says:

For the revelation awaits an appointed time; it speaks of the end and will not prove false. Though it lingers, wait for it; it will certainly come and will not delay.

(Habakkuk 2:3, NIV)

God is a faithful God. If you believe and you are convicted in Him, He will carry out His purpose in your life at His appointed time.

Faith in God and vision go hand-in-hand. Trials and tribulations are part of the roadmap that leads to fulfillment of purpose. Finding the reason for being coupled with accomplishing it is the true meaning of success. Instant gratification is suspended for the sake of vision that is geared towards self-discovery. The potential energy in an individual is activated into kinetic energy. An individual's actions with respect to time management are dictated by harbored vision. All available resources are deployed towards bringing forth the invisible to the visible.

To have vision is to have insight and focus on accomplishment of a specific purpose. This results in self-discipline, and with self-control choices are dictated by destiny. Life becomes simpler and narrower with vision. Decision-making becomes easier as there are fewer choices to pick from. For instance, with vision an individual chooses their relationships carefully. Interpersonal relationships are premised on the fulfillment of one's vision. With vision every passing second is spent on strategy that will bring about fulfillment of purpose.

An individual with vision has their private life In alignment with their public life. Their values and beliefs are in harmony with their behaviors. With vision a person has no difficulty in saying no to things that are not in line with purpose fulfillment.

Often, an unfocused person squanders time doing a good thing that is not congruent with their purpose. Important to note is that a *good* thing doesn't always translate into the best option. A good thing is not necessarily the right thing. It's important to note that when the devil fails to wear you out, the result is to preoccupy you with good things that are not in line with your destiny.

When your consciousness is dominated by positive thoughts that constitute your vision:

- You become someone who takes charge of their life.

- You come up with plans that dictate your actions.
- You set goals tactically and strategically that are geared towards fulfillment of your vision.
- You operate with the end in mind.
- You put first things first.
- You understand that success is preceded by having a fixed character as an individual.

A character of maturity and integrity is a must. The Spirit of God is our guide and teacher. He teaches us the ways of God, and helps us to adhere to Godly principles. This way our character is predictable and fixed. It's with the Spirit of God that revelation pertaining to our vision occurs. Our choices become limited to what is congruent with our vision. Instead of having our fingers in many pies, we focused on that one thing that is greater than the alternatives.

A lot of people are under the impression that there are a lot of things that we are obligated to do in life. However, vision makes it clear that significance lies in discovering *your gift*. Vision simplifies life as it eliminates the alternatives.

The power of vision is such that it truncates your options and dictates your decision-making. When you find God's purpose for your life, you find *you*. Your work on Earth is born out of a vision. Work is what you were born to do. It is the hidden potential that is exposed by vision. Adherence to a specific set of standards and behavior is paramount in living a purpose-driven life. Cultivating a spirit of tenacity, consistence, and commitment to fulfillment of your vision leads to genuine success.

Chapter 10:

Character is a Must

TO GET A better idea of how character is of importance and core to our success as a people requires first understanding its meaning. The word *character* traces its origin in the Greek language, and it means *an instrument used for engraving or carving.* However, before I delve deeper into what character is, let me talk about another word that is often used interchangeably with character.

Reputation is often mistaken for character. Reputation as a word has a Latin origin implying to consider, regard or think about. Therefore reputation refers to others' view of you.

Continuing, character refers to an engraver or instrument deployed for engraving. Engraving involves formation of permanent marks on a thing or object. In the same manner, a person cultivates character through engraving or carving out principles in his core that direct his behavior or habits. Character has more to do with the intrinsic, while reputation pertains to the extrinsic. With character a person's behavior or habits are fixed and unchanging. It defines one's philosophy of life which is a belief system organized around a steady set of intrinsic values that are in line with a person's purpose.

Fundamentally, character provides an individual a sense of self-identity and significance. A person of character embodies maturity and integrity—maturity in respect to emotional independence, implying that an individual's sense of security and self-worth is derived from within.

You don't have to depend on others' opinions or perceptions of you to feel worthy or secure. With character, the power to decide is dictated by your internal moral compass. This way an individual chooses to act in accordance with their values instead of reacting to circumstances.

The core of who we are is the spirit; therefore, character speaks to the principles that govern one's spirit.

Of importance is to seek the revelation of God's purpose for you. This is only possible through acceptance of Jesus Christ as your Lord and Savior. Then through cleansing, the Holy Spirit enters your heart to reveal God's purpose for your life. Because of guidance from the Spirit of God, your habits will be in congruence with Godly principles. An inside-out alignment with the right values and principles takes hold of your life. Hence a *person of character*.

Jesus never compromised on character. His private self was aligned with His public self. Jesus' character influenced and inspired masses and continues to do so up to this day.

One day as He preached, Jesus said:

"A good man brings good things out of the good stored up in his heart, and an evil man brings evil things

out of the evil stored up in his heart. For the mouth speaks what the heart is full of."

(Luke 6:45, NIV)

The essence of this is that when you speak you reveal what you really are because your words reflect who you are. And who you are speaks to your character.

Jesus added:

"As for everyone who comes to me and hears my words and puts them into practice, I will show you what they are like. They are like a man building a house, who dug down deep and laid the foundation on rock. When a flood came, the torrent struck that house but could not shake it, because it was well built."

(Luke 6: 48, NIV)

Important to note here is that without a doubt, character involves cultivating values in our core that produce "statue-like" habits and behaviors in a person. A person of positive character is one who doesn't seek validation from others, but draws on inner strength and security.

In event of financial or relationship stress, which is inevitable in life, character provides a fixed and unchanging foundation upon which purpose and potential are built. A person of character lives life that is dictated by principles geared towards fulfillment of purpose. Decision-making is centered around these principles. It's character that makes it possible to discover the leader trapped in each individual. Discovering the leader you are is about getting revelation of God's purpose for your life. And this revelation is only possible through restoration of the Holy Spirit in your life.

The scriptures assert that it's with the spirit that we serve God because God is Spirit. It's paramount for your spirit to commune with the Spirit of God so as to find out the original intent for your existence. The original intent for your existence is God's purpose for your life. In each individual God planted a seed and it's upon each of us to produce fruit from that seed. This is the very essence of being productive. Productivity translates into fulfillment of purpose, hence destiny. Destiny is protected by character. The character of an individual reflects their image.

In the Book of Genesis, it's asserted that God created man in His own image and likeness (Genesis 1:26), implying you have characteristics of God within you, and these characteristics should provide a basis for your character. Some of God's characteristics are love, kindness, and holiness which means parts of your spiritual DNA are love, kindness, and holiness. Omnipotent is one of the descriptions of God, and in a similar way man has an omnipotent nature too. This is evidenced in man's nature to create products through ideas, and imagination guided by the Spirit of God that reveals vision to man. As a human being, you should strive to be like God, that is, to have a character such as Jesus Christ.

In order for man to exercise dominion over all creation as instructed by God, having an image or character of God is a prerequisite. Image is character and vice versa. Character precedes dominion. To dominate your circumstances requires character to be in harmony with your purpose. That is, the principles that form the basis of your character should intersect with your behavior and habits. What am I saying? There should be a congruence between your values, actions, and behaviors so as to fulfill your God-chosen destiny.

With character comes self-control. Self-control is preceded by vision, and it is vision that produces specific plans and goals that enhance fulfillment of your purpose. When an individual lacks self-control, their character is flawed. In the words of Dag Hammarskjold[5]:

"You cannot play with the animal in you without becoming wholly animal, play with falsehood without forfeiting your right to truth, play with cruelty without losing your sensitivity of mind. He who wants to

---

[5] Swedish diplomat, economist, and author (1905-1961) — Wikipedia

*keep his garden tidy doesn't reserve
a plot for weeds."*

A person of character is not a hypocrite. A hypocrite is defined by Webster's Dictionary as a person who acts in contradiction to his or her stated beliefs or feelings. Such a person says one thing and does another. Therefore, character is about being consistent no matter what. In the face of trials, tribulation, and adversity, a person of character is still standing. Character is built or developed out of a vision to fulfill one's destiny. Character is not something handed down to you from God. Character involves a gradual process that entails values cultivated over a period of time.

These values produce morals and ethics that define your behavior. Integrity and dignity are born out of one's behavior. A person of integrity is uncompromising on honesty and trust. Integrity is defined by Webster's Dictionary as the quality or state of being complete and undivided. Therefore, character is predicated on oneness. Oneness is the main characteristic of God, because He is unchanging and the same yesterday, today, and forever. That's why we trust God. In the same way a person of character is easily trusted by others.

Integrity is so important to God that He prefers you to have an intact integrity (which is character), even if it comes down to losing everything in your life. God is glorified when you demonstrate character and remain aligned to Him, amidst temptations, trials, or tests.

The Book of Job corroborates the importance of weathering the storms of life, no matter what. An excerpt is as follows:

Have you not put a hedge around him and his household and everything he has? You have blessed the work of his hands, so that his flocks and herds are spread throughout the land. But now stretch out your hand and strike everything he has, and he will surely curse You to Your face.

(Job 1:10-11, NIV)

The Lord said to Satan, "Very well then, everything he has is in your power, but on the man himself do not lay a finger." Then Satan went out from the presence of the Lord.

(Job 1: 12, NIV)

The devil proceeded to wreak havoc in Job's life, ranging from destruction of property to death of his children. It was total decimation of Job; however, he remained steadfast, and faithful to God. Talk about epitomizing character. Come hell or high water, rain or shine, Job was still standing.

The Scripture says:

Naked I came from my mother's womb, and naked I will depart. The Lord gave and the Lord has taken away; may the name of the Lord be praised.

(Job 1:21, NIV)

Without a doubt, Job still trusted God. Trust is a product of character. Character preserves integrity. It's character that narrows your scope of decision-making. That is, your goals and objectives are lucid. This translates into a life that is fulfilling and purposeful.

Chapter 11:

The Power of Passion

I AM REMINDED of a co-worker who happened to complain of not feeling well one evening. He couldn't exactly pinpoint what the issue was. He sought help at the workplace clinic and after assessment of his vital signs by the nurse, his blood pressure and heart rate were found to be within normal range. Later on that evening he was allowed to leave work before shift end by his supervisor. Three days later he was absent from work without notice. His supervisor endeavored to reach him, but in vain. Nearby hospitals were reached to determine if he happened to be admitted, but to no avail.

Next, police were notified of this disturbing and uncertain situation surrounding the absence of this co-worker. When the police got to his place of residence, they had to forcibly open the door to access his house. On entering his house, he was found dead in his bathroom. The autopsy confirmed a heart attack as the cause of death.

The deceased had given twenty years of his life to this company. I wondered if this job was his passion.

Because of the unpredictable nature of incidents like this, and the fleeting nature of time coupled with the uncertainty of life itself, it's imperative to approach life with passion of purpose. But what really is passion?

Passion is originally derived from the Latin word *passio* which implies *suffering*. In this regard, historically and presently, it's associated with the suffering of Jesus Christ between the Passover and crucifixion. This moment in time is referred to as the Passion of Christ. Christ Jesus was an embodiment of passion. He endured intense suffering; however, He remained steadfast, unyielding, and persistent in fulfilling his purpose. Therefore, in the true sense of the word, to be passionate about purpose is to remain committed to fulfilling the reason for existence.

Irrespective of trials, tests, and tribulations, a passionate individual doesn't lose enthusiasm in the face of resistance. Passion is about remaining enthusiastic about the desire to fulfill a dream in the face of one failure after another. It's important to understand that failure is part of the process called life. However, many a people are afraid to try because of the fear of failure. Yet the greatest tragedy is dying without having ever thrown your weight behind anything. Many a people prefer to choose a path of least resistance. But with passion you muster the courage to go where there is no path and make one.

Passion is the loss of terror of opposition, and a drive for a strong desire to fulfill your purpose. A passionate individual is like a rock in the ocean. Hurricanes come and go, tsunamis come and go, currents come and go; however, the rock remains standing.

It is passion that drove the little-known and young country pastor from Dexter Avenue Baptist Church in Alabama to headline the Montgomery bus boycott. After being chosen to lead the bus boycott, Dr. Martin Luther King Jr. said:

> *"We have no alternative but to protest. For many years we have shown an amazing patience ... but we come here tonight to be saved from that patience that makes us patient with anything less than freedom and justice."*

Dedication to passion for purpose is what made Nelson Mandela give up his career as an attorney to become a warrior of freedom and equality for all. On several occasions, he was arrested and stood trial. Mandela was incarcerated for 27 years, but was still believing.

A passionate individual understands that pain is temporary. Pain is part of the process and after the pain is your reward. To operate at this level requires communing of your spirit with the Spirit of God. In the words of Prophet Isaiah:

When you pass through the waters, I will be with you, and when you pass through the rivers, they will not sweep you over. When you walk through the fire, you will not be burned; the flames will not set you ablaze.

(Isaiah 43:2, NIV)

Passion breeds self-control as well as self-discipline in that an individual's options are narrowed to choices that correlate with vision and purpose fulfillment. Because of limited choices that are aligned with an individual's goals and objectives, time management is efficient. Proper planning of time allows a passionate person to effectively make the best use of every passing hour. By nature time is fleeting, and passion makes you invest your time in activities that contribute to your desired end. A passionate individual understands that success is only possible through the wise use of time.

To a passionate individual success is about putting everything on the line for a particular cause or goal, the accomplishment of which brings about a sense of fulfillment. Many a people tend to understand success from a worldly perspective of fame, power, prominence, and money accumulation. Not so with a person passionate about his desired end. Passion makes you understand that true success is what you accomplish juxtaposed upon what you set out to achieve. It has no relation to what others achieve or accomplish.

Passion provides a clear perspective that you truly succeed when you meet the requirements of the original idea. This is important so as to live a life of fulfillment.

So if success is fulfillment of the original idea to a passionate individual, then understanding one's reason for existence is crucial to a person who embodies passion. This makes one realize the only way to know the reason for existence is by seeking the Spirit of God for guidance. It's with the Holy Spirit that you get a revelation of your hidden gift or talents. It's with the Spirit of God that the dormant power in you is activated to reach the purpose for which you were created. Passion keeps you going irrespective of the trials and tests that you encounter. Passion is the heart that beats in rhythm with the Spirit of God.

With the Spirit of God's guidance, the winds of change are effectively handled by a passionate individual. Change is inevitable, and it's part of the life process. Passion instills fortitude, courage, and resilience to cope with the currents of change. Change is one of the constants that every individual encounters during the course of their life. It's paramount to acknowledge this fact, and then live with the expectation of change. This insulates you from descending into a sense of feeling overwhelmed by life's circumstances. Instead of asking "Why me?" you ask "What can I do about this?" each time you are confronted with change.

A passionate individual is convicted that somehow, some way, change is here to serve me.

Now let me state unequivocally that not all passion will lead to productivity. Every human walking the face of Earth harbors a passion of some sort; however, only passion that is in alignment with God's purpose produces personal fulfillment. No matter how passionate you are, and how good of a vision you have, you can't reap the fruit of true success disconnected from the Spirit of God. It's the Spirit of God that is a conduit to revelation of your God given-gifts and talents. The Spirit of God connection to your spirit is the key to a rewarding and fulfilling life.

The Apostle Paul says:

These are the things God has revealed to us by His Spirit. The Spirit searches all things, even the deep things of God. For who knows a person's thought except their own spirit within them? In the same way no one knows the thoughts of God except the Spirit of God.

(1 Corinthians 2:10-11, NIV)

This is so crucial; it means that the only way to know the secrets of God about your life is through communion of your spirit with the Spirit of God.

So passion in seeking deeper relationship with God is of essence. It's God the Creator of you, the God who designed you that is so conversant of your purpose.

God has so much in store for you that your mind can't comprehend it. In the words of Paul the Apostle:

However, as it is written: What no eye has seen, what no ear has heard, and what no human mind has conceived - the things God has prepared for those who love Him.

(1 Corinthians 2: 9, NIV)

God is the source of all things. Therefore, through discernment the Spirit of God reveals to you what God has in store for you. Important to note is that only through obedience to God, and desisting from acts of sin can we reap and enjoy the fruit of genuine success that glorifies God's name.

Jesus said:

I am the true vine, and my Father is the gardener. He cuts off every branch in Me that bears no fruit, while every branch that does bear fruit He prunes so that it will bear even more fruit.

Here Christ Jesus confirms He is the source you should turn to if you are going to bear fruit. Then Jesus added:

Remain in me, as I also remain in you. No branch can bear fruit by itself; it must remain in the vine. Neither can you bear fruit unless you remain in me.

(John 15: 4, NIV)

Without mincing words, Christ Jesus emphatically and categorically makes it known that you can't experience personal fulfillment if you are not connected to Him.

Passion that is rooted in God's purpose for your life will be the only kind that leads to victory. Seeking a deeper connection and meaning with Christ Jesus is key to understanding your reason for existence.

Remember that God created you to rule Earth on His behalf. You have the mandate from the Most High to dominate and subdue your circumstances. If you are being dominated by life itself, then you have to turn back to the Creator. Accept Jesus as your personal Lord and Savior and commit to fulfilling God's purpose for your life. Remain passionate in executing your reason for existence. God will provide anything you need that is in line with fulfillment of His purpose for your life.

Chapter 12:

Change is a Part of the Process

CHANGE IS everywhere and massive change is happening around the world. Glaciers in the coldest places on Earth are melting. Politically, leadership in various countries changes daily. The global population has been changing and on the rise since the creation of first man, Adam. Pandemics like COVID-19 are impacting the world and changing our way of life. If there is one thing that is consistent, constant, and permanent, it is change. Success or failure is premised on how well you handle change. Therefore, it's important to embrace change through preparing and planning.

Midway through the year of 2021, my mom was diagnosed with a serious type of cancer. Anticipating the loss of my mom due to the serious illness created storms of worry in my mind. Trying to wrap my head around this matter was tough to bear. I was tormented by the anticipation of this uncertainty, a change I had no control over. The fear of losing her overwhelmed me sometimes, even with the knowledge that change is part and parcel of life.

Two days to Christmas that year, Mom passed on. I was numbed by her loss and felt out of balance for a while. However, understanding that change is inevitable and can't be prevented from happening helped me to adapt to the new normal.

Marcus Aurelius, a Roman Emperor once said:

Observe constantly that all things take place by change, and accustom thyself to consider that the nature of the Universe loves nothing so much as to change the things which are, and to make new things like them.

In other words, change is a constant presence in life, and many a people are aware of this. However, countless humans tend to resist change if not fear it. Great individuals perceive that change presents opportunities. Actually, the default setting of the human brain is to keep you in what is normal to you. To keep you in a predictable environment, so to speak. However, the courage to step outside the norm will bring about the change we desire.

Like time, change is a factor of life that cannot be stopped. The Merriam-Webster's Dictionary defines change as something becoming different, or to undergo transformation or transition. Transitions happen all the time and never end. For instance, transiting from childhood to adulthood, from student to professional, from being single to being married, from one job to another, from marriage to divorce, ad infinitum.

Change dominates life, it impacts both living things and nonliving things. Nature keeps changing as well. At one point the sun is shining, the next minute it's raining. The fact is change is unavoidable.

In the words of Aurelius:

Is any man afraid of change? What can take place without change? What then is more pleasing or more suitable to the universal nature? And can you take a hot bath unless the wood for the fire undergoes a change? And can you be nourished unless the food undergoes a change? And can anything else that is useful be accomplished without change? Do you not see then that for yourself also to change is just the same, and equally necessary for the universal nature?

Important to note here is that change is beneficial to our well-being and not always adverse.

The creation of the heavens and universe was a process premised on change. God brought about change through the word. God spoke for six days to bring about His creation that included mountains, rivers, vegetation, animals, man, ad infinitum. Change was part and parcel of the creation, and still is ever present. The very existence of humankind is premised on switching from eternity to time, and back to eternity. Rotation of the earth along its axis and around the sun brings about night and day—change, so to speak. Hence change is a powerful force that impacts humankind in every way imaginable.

Along the continuum of life our own bodies experience changes as we go through the process of development and maturation. That aside, change in our relationships is inevitable as well as change in our friends. People come into our lives and people walk out of our lives. Nothing wrong with this, the important thing is to understand their part in your story is determined by God.

Another change you experience is that of knowledge and understanding. This is evidenced by the variation in our values and interests. For instance, what used to interest you as a teenager no longer matters in adulthood. Hence your priorities and interests change as you grow.

Continuing, the Bible says:

As long as the earth endures, seedtime and harvest, cold and heat, summer and winter, day and night will never cease.

(Genesis 8:22, NIV)

God makes it crystal clear that change is part and parcel of life. The understanding of this can help you have a positive view of change; however, it may not necessarily allay the fear that is associated with change. Many a people have an inherent desire to resist change. They prefer a comfortable environment where everything is predictable. However, this is not always the case. To live with the expectation that things will always be the same is setting yourself up for frustration and disappointment.

I am here to report that growing as an individual and experiencing personal fulfillment happens *outside* a comfortable environment. It's in an environment where unpredictability reigns that growth and personal fulfillment occurs. The courage to step into the unknown is a prerequisite towards accomplishment of God's purpose for your life. This calls for practical faith in God.

The Bible says:

In their hearts humans plan their course, but the Lord establishes their steps.

(Proverbs 16:9, NIV)

The essence of this is that you are responsible for coming up with the plans that will lead to your success. And as you implement the plans God will guide you step-by-step, by His Spirit.

Of importance is how you handle or respond to change—and better still, how you prepare for change. To ignore change is counterproductive. Turning a blind eye doesn't stop change or prevent you from being impacted by change. To bury your head in the sand in a bid to ignore or refuse to address the inevitable is not a win-win solution.

The first step in dealing effectively with change is acknowledgement of the ubiquitous nature of change—to accept that it is present everywhere, and all over the place. To understand change is inescapable is an important step in the right direction. But accepting change shouldn't be in the sense of surrendering to it, but adapting or adjusting to it.

The Apostle Paul says:

Do not conform to the pattern of this world, but be he transformed by the renewing of your mind. Then you will be able to test and approve what God's will is - his good, pleasing and perfect will.

(Romans 12:2, NIV)

The crux of this matter is that transformation is only possible through the mind. How you think, plan, and prepare is key to effectively managing change. When you prepare and plan for change, in effect you avoid becoming a victim of change. Planning for change is predicated on the foundation of the expectation of change. It's living with the expectation that things will not always remain the same.

So the genesis of planning is born out of thoughts. God will always allow us to have thoughts that are in line with our destiny. The Scripture says that as a man thinketh in his heart so is he. (Proverbs 23:7). Creative thinking generates ideas which bring about objectives and goals. Then the possible course of action is incubated from ideas. Ideas give rise to mental pictures or representations that are invisible and not yet reality. These mental representations occur in the subconscious mind (heart in scripture), the ultimate center of imagination. When it comes to imagination the subconscious mind can't separate reality from imagination. It is this imagination put on paper that provides a plan to follow in preparing for change.

Jeremiah the prophet asserts:

For I know the plans I have for you,
declares the Lord. Plans to prosper
you and not to harm you, plans to
give you hope and a future.

(Jeremiah 29:11, NIV)

God Himself corroborates that your future is already planned, implying that a roadmap towards your destination is present. So if God relies on a plan to bring about your future fulfillment, then it's obvious that planning is paramount in dealing with the unknown that is the future. This unknown is filled with the winds of change and time not yet used.

Success in handling and dealing with change is entirely premised on planning. Without proper planning, change will destroy your life, visions, or dreams. To be able to control change is only possible through the planning process.

Isaiah says:

But the noble make noble plans,
and by noble deeds they stand.

(Isaiah 32:8, NIV)

In times of difficulty and uncertainty, a clear plan is always relied on for direction. A good plan becomes the benchmark against which decisions are made, a point of reference to weather change, so to speak.

The path to genuine success and personal fulfillment is full of change. Of importance is to be aware of and to live with the expectation that change is inevitable. You have to be ready and prepared for the unknown or unexpected. In doing this you rest and sit in God. You have to have faith in yourself and in God. Planning in its very nature is predicated on faith. It's soothing to know that no situation is permanent.

King Solomon asserts:

There is a time for everything, and a season for every activity under the heavens.

(Ecclesiastes 3:1, NIV)

With persistence and commitment you will outlast every situation on your way to real success and personal fulfillment.

Conclusion

Let us make mankind in our image and likeness so that they may rule over the fish in the sea and birds in the sky, over the livestock and all the creatures that move along the ground.

(Genesis 1:26)

THESE ARE NOT my words, nope! This is testament from God our Father. You and I were born to rule, to have dominion over God's creation, actually.

This is God's mandate for mankind, and it's your calling. Now you may ask, "How do I exercise dominion?" Look no further than Genesis 1:28. In clear and precise terms, the Lord Almighty commanded us to be fruitful, to multiply, to replenish, and to subdue, And when we do this, dominion is realized.

Now, to be fruitful is more about being productive—productivity in one's areas of gifting so to speak. This kind of productivity is geared towards creating something of value that benefits others. For instance, when Steve Jobs created the iPhone, it was for the benefit of others. After producing the iPhone, he multiplied it by reproducing millions of them. Then the iPhone was replenished through distribution, resulting in subduing the smart phone market. Arguably, Apple the iPhone maker is the most valuable company in the world. This is the exemplar of dominion. I can say with confidence that Steve Jobs discovered his purpose, which then translated into personal fulfillment. He had a vision, not ambition, to make humanity better. And you too were created to fulfill a specific purpose.

God had to interrupt eternity to bring you into the concept of time with two definitive boundaries: birth and death. Between being born and dying is a duration in which you have to discover your original reason for existence which is purpose. Between being born and dying exists a chance for you and me to tap into our hidden gifts and talents to realize our true potential. Potential is the dormant ability that is common to all of us. However, potential requires activation.

Faith in God and courage to change what we can are necessary for activation of one' s potential. Harnessing of potential produces the reason for your existence which is your God-given purpose. In Proverbs 19:21 it is written that many are the plans in a person's heart, but it is the Lord's purpose that prevails. Simply put, God's purpose stands no matter what. Therefore, it's of utmost importance to discover this purpose.

Why? Because true and genuine success is the fulfillment of God's purpose for your life.

About the Author

ROBERT MULINDWA is an author, speaker, and transformational voice dedicated to awakening human potential through wisdom, identity, and conscious living. His work centers on a single conviction: that sustainable success, wealth, and fulfillment flow not from external striving, but from rediscovering who we truly are.

He is the author of three books, including *Created for Success*, an Amazon Best Seller that challenges conventional definitions of achievement and calls readers back to their original design. His second work, *Rediscovering Identity*, explores the crisis of selfhood in modern society and the quiet power that emerges when individuals remember their true essence. His latest book, *Gain Wisdom, Gain Wealth*, synthesizes timeless principles with practical insight, revealing wisdom as the ultimate currency behind lasting prosperity. Robert's perspective is uniquely shaped by a rare convergence of disciplines. He holds a Bachelor of Science in Statistics, an MBA in Financial Management and Investment, and is also a Registered Nurse. This uncommon blend of analytical rigor, financial acumen, and human-centered care informs his ability to speak with both precision and depth—bridging mind, money, and meaning.

Beyond credentials and publications, Robert is a husband and father whose life philosophy is lived, not merely taught. His message is rooted in the belief that when individuals realign with their true nature, clarity replaces confusion, order replaces struggle, and purpose replaces noise. Currently based in Nashville, Tennessee, Robert is building a media company devoted to transforming mindsets one person at a time. Through books, digital media, and spoken word, his expanding platform challenges inherited limitations, dissolves false narratives, and reintroduces wisdom as the foundation of personal and collective advancement. Robert Mulindwa's work does not seek to add something new to the individual—but to remove what was never true. His voice stands at the intersection of insight and awakening, reminding audiences that the greatest breakthrough is not becoming more, but remembering who you already are.

To reach Robert about speaking, appearances, quantity discounts on books, and other matters, please visit:

www.RobertMulindwa.com

Find Your Freedom

**Want to know how to get started
on your own path?**

You've finished the book, but your journey is just beginning. Go further toward fulfillment and find out more about the I AM Movement:

- Sign up for the *I AM Newsletter* and get your free **12 Tips for Successfully Starting A Life-Changing Journey Within.**

- Find out about upcoming **webinars**, **challenges**, and **speaking** engagements.

- Apply for 1-on-1 **Coaching.**

Choose your next step, visit:

www.RobertMulindwa.com

Thank You

I SINCERELY HOPE you enjoyed *Created for Success* as much as I enjoyed writing it, and that it does help you achieve a more successful future, one guided by God's will and filled with fulfilment and purpose.

You could have picked any book, but you picked mine, and for that I'm grateful. I hope it added value and quality to your life. If so, it would be really nice if you could share this book with your colleagues, friends, and family. It may help them as well. You might post a review or your thoughts with your favorite place to buy books or social media, and/or simply recommend it to someone.

Your feedback and support will help me improve my craft and fill my heart.

Thank you!

Robert Mulindwa

Notes

Introduction

1. http://www.unfpa.org/data/world-population-dashboard.
2. http://www.merriam-webster.com/dictionary.

Chapter 1

3. http://www.reuters.com/article/us-merckle-newsmaker-sb/german-billionaire-commits-suicide-after-vw-losses.
4. Myles Munroe, *Understanding your Place in God's Kingdom.*

Chapter 2

5. http://www.crosswalk.com/author/carrie-lowrance.
6. Myles Munroe, *Discover the Hidden You.*

Chapter 3

7. http://www.gotquestions.org/Bible-time-management.
8. http://www.goodreads.com.
9. Myles Munroe, *Becoming a Leader.*
10. Munroe, *Understanding Your Place in God's Kingdom.*

Chapter 4

11. http://www.uschamber.com>strategy.
12. http://www.nm.org>healthy-tips.
13. Tony Robbins, *Awaken the Giant Within.*

CHAPTER FIVE

14. http://www.gettysburg.edu.
15. http://www.marketwatch.com/people-are-spending-most-of-their-waking- hours-staring-at-screens.
16. http://www.dictionary.com.

CHAPTER SIX

17. http://www.merriam-webster.com/dictionary.
18. Nelson Mandela, *Long Walk to Freedom: The Autobiography of Nelson Mandela.*

CHAPTER SEVEN

19. http://www.adamsmith.org.
20. Myles Munroe, *The Purpose and Power of The Holy Spirit: God's Government on Earth.*

CHAPTER EIGHT

21. http://www.sandiego.edu>news>details.
22. Munroe, *Becoming a Leader.*

CHAPTER NINE

23. http://www.merriam-webster.com/dictionary.
24. http://www.sil.si.edu/ondisplay/langley/intro.htm.

25. http://www.history.com/topics/invetions/wright-brothers.

CHAPTER TEN

26. http://www.bibletools.org/index.cfm/fuseaction/lexicon.show/ID/G5481/character.htm.
27. http://www.etymologeek.com/eng/reputation.
28. http://www.merriam-webster.com.
29. http://www.slife.org>dag-hammarskjold.

CHAPTER ELEVEN

30. http://onceuponawrittenword.wordpress.com/2018/2/19/the-metamorphosis-of-passion.
31. http://www.kansascity.com>local.
32. Mandela, *Long Walk to Freedom: The Autobiography of Nelson Mandela*.

CHAPTER TWELVE

33. http://www.merriam-webster.com/dictionary.
34. http://www.orionphilosophy.com
35. http://www.azquotes.com.